Asian Martial Arts, Monks, and Ways of Thought

An Anthology from the Journal of Asian Martial Arts
compiled by Michael A. DeMarco, M.A.

Disclaimer
Please note that the authors and publisher of this book are not responsible in any manner whatsoever for any injury that may result from practicing the techniques and/or following the instructions given within. Since the physical activities described herein may be too strenuous in nature for some readers to engage in safely, it is essential that a physician be consulted prior to training.

All Rights Reserved
No part of this publication, including illustrations, may be reproduced or utilized in any form or by any means, electronic or mechanical, including photocopying, recording, or by any information storage and retrieval system (beyond that copying permitted by sections 107 and 108 of the US Copyright Law and except by reviewers for the public press), without written permission from Via Media Publishing Company.

Warning: Any unauthorized act in relation to a copyright work may result in both a civil claim for damages and criminal prosecution.

Copyright © 2020
by Via Media Publishing Company

Articles in this anthology were originally published in the *Journal of Asian Martial Arts*. Listed according to the table of contents for this anthology:

Spiesbach, M. (1992), Vol. 1 No. 4, pp. 10–27
Holcombe, C. (1993), Vol. 2 No. 1, pp. 10-25
Shine, J. (1993), Vol. 2 No. 1, pp. 84–91
Wiley, M. (1994), Vol. 3 No. 4, pp. 38–45
Henning, S. (1998), Vol. 7 No. 1, pp. 90–101
Hawthorne, R. (2000), Vol. 9 No. 1, pp. 70–81
Jerimiah, K. (2007), Vol. 16 No. 2, pp. 18–33
Kelland, S. (2009), Vol. 18 No. 3, pp. 8–17

Cover Illustrations
Monk practicing in front of the main gate of Shaolin Temple.
Background: Kiyumizu Temple.
Photography by Shkufu. Courtesy of Creative Commons, CC BY-SA 4.0
https://creativecommons.org/about/downloads/ Public Domain.
Background photography, cCourtesy of www.pxfuel.com.

Print Edition
ISBN-13: 9798562576958

www.viamediapublishing.com

contents

iv Preface
    by Michael DeMarco, M.A.

CHAPTERS

1   Bodhidharma: Meditating Monk,
    Martial Arts Master or Make-Believe?
    by Michael Spiesbach, M.A., J.D.

25 The Daoist Origins of the Chinese Martial Arts
    by Charles Holcombe, Ph.D.

45 Sohei: The Warrior Monks of Old Japan
    by Jerry Shine

53 Silat Kebatinan as an Expression of Mysticism
    and Martial Culture in Southeast Asia
    by Mark V. Wiley

64 Reflections on a Visit to the Shaolin Monastery
    by Stanley E. Henning, M.A.

79 Reviving the Daoist Roots of Internal Martial Arts
    by Mark Hawthorne

91 Asceticism and the Pursuit of Death by Warriors and Monks
    by Ken Jeremiah, M.A.

141 Psychology, Physical Disability, and the Application
    of Buddhist Mindfulness to Martial Arts Programs
    by Mark D. Kelland, Ph.D.

125 Index

preface

Many know of the legends concerning the Shaolin Temple as the font of Asian martial arts. However, this was not the only temple with deep associations with combatives. This anthology dives deep into the historic significance of the relationship between temples, monks, and martial arts.

As a transporter of culture, it seems logical that the Indian monk Bodhidharma brought more than just Buddhist texts to the Shaolin Temple. India has a wonderful tradition of martial and healing arts that he would have shared at the temple. His rich story throws light on how and why monks throughout Asia have often blended martial arts with their spiritual lives.

Asian countries have unique histories and societies, but also share important elements. A major thread is religion and the mixing with ancient native shamanism and mysticism. We find a blend of Buddhism, Daoism, Confucianism, Hinduism, and Islam in Asian cultures, which are strongly based in monastic centers. The spread of religious thought is coupled with the spread of knowledge about martial arts. It is part of human nature to find sources to enforce the spiritual, mental, and physical condition. Temples and martial arts are certainly valued for these reasons.

In the first chapter, Michael Spiesbach details the story of Bodhidharma. His piece couples nicely with Stanley Henning's observations from a visit to the Shaolin Temple. Dr. Charles Holcombe details the historic connections Daoism has with martial arts, while Mark Hawthorne discusses the recent state of Daoism and its prospects for the future.

Jerry Shine's chapter on the *sohei* shows the influence these warrior monks had in Japanese history. Ken Jeremiah's chapter looks at the extreme asceticism Japanese monks and warriors practiced to reach their individual goals. Mark Wiley's chapter deals with mystical elements as sources of power in Indonesian martial arts. In the final chapter, Mark Kelland brings the religious and martial traditions into our present everyday lives.

Michael A. DeMarco, Publisher
Santa Fe, New Mexico, November 2020

chapter 1

Bodhidharma:
Meditating Monk, Martial Arts Master or Make-Believe?

by Michael Spiesbach, M.A., J.D.

According to tradition, Bodhidharma crossed the Yangtze River by standing on a reed. Another version says this is how he crossed the Sea of Japan. Photo courtesy of Steven Scherling.

Most Western students of Asian martial arts, if they have done any research on the subject at all, will surely have come across references to Bodhidharma. He is known in Chinese as *Putidamo* (often abbreviated to *Damo*), in Japan as *Daruma*, and in Korea as *Dalmadaisa*. As often as not, this Indian Buddhist monk is cited as the primal source for all martial arts styles or, at the very least, for any style which traces its roots back to the fabled Shaolin Temple. However, the question of his contributions to the martial arts and to Zen (Chan or Ch'an) Buddhism and even of his very existence has been a matter of controversy among historians and martial arts scholars for many years. Some believe there is little doubt that such an individual came from India to "evangelize" China with Mahayana Buddhism. One has even definitively stated that "the existence of Bodhidharma can not be doubted . . ." (Lanciotti, 1949: 141). Others feel he was created as an amalgam of those principles later Chan patriarchs and practitioners wanted retroactively to connect with the Buddha.

In order to fully understand Bodhidharma and before one can look at him from a martial arts perspective, one must first understand his significance to Chan Buddhism. Historical references to Bodhidharma begin with the *Luoyang jia lan ji*. Authored by Yang Xuanzhi in 547 C.E., it is the earliest known work to mention a Bodhidharma. This document, "The History of the Monasteries of Luoyang," tells of its author making his way to the Yong Ning Temple where there was living a "barbarian" called Sramana Bodhidharma from the Bosi region (Persia), who stated that he was 150 years old.

After the *Luoyang*, there was little written about Bodhidharma during the following centuries. Guifeng Zongni (780-841 C.E.) does mention a person by that name in the "Preface to the Complete Explanation of the Source of Chan," in explaining the *gongan* (*koan*) "Why did Bodhidharma come from the West?" (Chang, 1969: 86). However, it is interesting that the seventh century historian, Xuan Zhuang, who visited both Bodhidharma's purported birthplace and the Shaolin Temple fails to even mention him (Reid, 1984: 27).

Notwithstanding the *Luoyang*, there are actually only two reliable sources regarding Bodhidharma's life. The first is the *Xu gao seng zhuan* or the "Biographies of Eminent Tang Monks," written by Dao Xuan in 645 C.E. during the early Tang Dynasty. Dao Xuan was the founder of the Vinaya sect in China and a scholar. The *Biographies* was written centuries before Chan came to maturity in China and is the first record of Bodhidharma's life. At that time there were many known Buddhist meditation (*dhyana*) practitioners, but it was someone called Seng Zhou, not Bodhidharma, who was renowned as the greatest dhyana expert east of the Himalayas. Bodhidharma was mentioned only because he practiced Mahayana (greater vehicle Buddhism) meditation, not Hinayana (lesser vehicle Buddhism). Amazingly, for someone who supposedly abjured writings, Dao Xuan states that Bodhidharma wrote down his words so they might be transmitted to the world (Suzuki, 1978: 178-83).

Many writings throughout the centuries have been attributed to Bodhidharma, likely due in no small part to Dao Xuan's statement. At various times scholars have credited Bodhidharma as the author of numerous works. One such, the *Er ru si xing lun* ("Discourse on the Twofold Entrance to the Way and the Four Types of Practice"), describes a Zen approach to how to become enlightened to the fundamental spirit of Buddhism. The actual author is unknown, but it is now certain that he was not Bodhidharma, and, it appeared 200 years after his death (Barnet and Burto, 1982: 9 and 28). It is recognized as a reference only because from it has come the most famous and cogent expression of Chan, which is universally attributed to Bodhidharma:

> A special transmission outside the scriptures;
> No dependence upon words or letters;
> Direct pointing at the soul of man;
> Seeing into one's nature.

The current scholarly consensus is that all writings attributed to Bodhidharma are spurious and that later Chan priests beginning in about the eighth century put words into Bodhidharma's mouth. Until proven otherwise, a conservative position requires agreement with this view.

The other important work mentioning Bodhidharma is the *Jing de zhuan deng tu*, or "The Records of Transmission of the Lamp," compiled by Dao Yuan in 1004 C.E. It is the earliest historical record of Chan Buddhism and contains over one thousand gongan, the names of over one thousand Chan masters and the sayings of some six hundred of these masters, all in thirty volumes. It devotes an entire fascicle to Bodhidharma. Zen scholar Daisetz Suzuki believed that the greater part of the *Records* is historical. His reasoning was based in part upon the fact that Dao Yuan was a Chan monk who wrote his work after the full flowering of Chan in China (Suzuki, 1978: 178). However, as another Zen scholar has more recently concluded, there is just as much reason to doubt the *Records*, since they are "historically unreliable" (Dumoulin, 1963: 159). The *Records* mentions the Temple of Perfect Peace (which is also described in the *Luoyang*) as the place where Bodhidharma was supposed to have been when he stated that he was 150 years old. From these references, it has been deduced that Bodhidharma was in *Luoyang* during the period of the temple's greatest prosperity, i.e., between 516 and 526 C.E. Importantly, the *Records* also mentions practice of *biguan* ("wall gazing" meditation).

Mainstream tradition holds that Bodhidharma arrived in China in the year 520 C.E. This date is based upon "An Essay on The Orthodox Transmission of the Dharma" written by Qi Song during the Song Dynasty (360-1250 C.E.) (Suzuki, 1969: 9). There are some indications, however, that he arrived in China many years prior to that time, in 470 C.E. or even as early as 420 C.E. The *Biographies* state that Bodhidharma began to travel through the region of the Liu Song before the fall of that dynasty, which occurred in 479 C.E. At any rate, it appears that if he did come to China, it was likely not later than 520 C.E.

There is also no unanimity as to where Bodhidharma first arrived in China nor by which route he traveled. Some scholars, following the account in the *Records*, state that he traveled by sea, arriving at modern day Nanjing, the Liang Dynasty's capital from 502-556 C.E. He is said to have embarked from Madras in Southern India, "risking his life over the towering waves of the Southern Seas" (Suzuki, 1982: 23), by sailing to modern Guangzhou and then traveling by land up to Nanjing. Some contemporary writers say the trip took three years (Hakuyu and Glassman, 1976: 85; Sekida, 1983: 36-37) and caused him to travel over 100,000 *li* (approximately 33,000 miles by ancient Chinese standards).

Other scholars feel that he walked to China, following "what was in those days a well-beaten trail" (Hoover, 1978: 3). One even outlines this "northern route" as "over the Pamir plateau through Chinese Turkistan, across the desert and along the course of the Yellow River down to the city of Luoyang, at the eastern head of the Yellow River. Luoyang was the capital of Wei, and at the time was the center of culture and Buddhist activities" (Ross, 1966: 57). This journey from India, whether over land or by sea, was long and dangerous.

Bodhidharma was supposedly born in Kanchipuram (or Conjerveem) near Madras, the third son of a king from Southern India and thus a member of the *kshatriya* caste (warriors and rulers). His date of birth is subject to varying estimates: 448 and 470 C.E. are among those often cited. At the age of seven he purportedly stated that "mind is a jewel." At that time, his teacher Prajnatara (sometimes referred to as Hannyatara), the twenty-seventh Patriarch of Chan Buddhism, changed the boy's name from Bodhitara to Bodhidharma. After his father's death, Bodhidharma served Prajnatara for forty years, propagating Buddhism against indigenous Indian philosophy. At the age of 110, after Prajnatara's death, he left his monastery in India for China, following Prajnatara's exhortation to go there and spread the Teaching (Hakuyu and Glassman, 1976: 71-74 and 85).

There are three major incidents connected with his years in China:

1) a dialogue with Liang Dynasty Emperor Wu Di, 2) his nine-year biguan meditation, and 3) a meeting at the Shaolin Temple with his successor, Hui Ke. Historians almost universally play down his relationship to the martial arts as minor or, more often, fail to mention it at all.

Bodhidharma's famous dialogue with Emperor Wu Di is neither regarded as historical fact by most scholars nor mentioned in the *Luoyang* or the *Biographies*. In fact, the story did not appear until several hundred years after the event in question was suppose.d to have happened. While this would seem to confirm that it is a legend, it nonetheless exemplifies a central facet of Chan Buddhism. According to Chan tradition, Bodhidharma had an audience with Emperor Wu Di (465-550 C.E.), who originally had persecuted Buddhists but after a Pauline conversion embraced and promoted the religion. After taking Buddhist vows, he turned to persecuting Daoists. He ruled from Nanjing and, because of his patronage, made it the prime center for Buddhist learning in China. Most versions of the meeting follow the same script. The Emperor invited Bodhidharma to his court where the following exchange supposedly took place with the Emperor asking Bodhidharma:

> "Since my enthronement, I have had many monasteries built and had many holy writings copied as well as vested many priests and nuns. How great is the merit that is due to me?"
> "No merit at all," was the response from Bodhidharma.
> "What is the Noble Truth in its highest sense?" then asked the Emperor.
> "It is empty. No nobility whatever," replied Bodhidharma.
> The Emperor then inquired, "Who is it then that is facing me?"
> Bodhidharma answered, "I do not know, Sire."

As stated, in all probability this event never happened. The purpose of the story was, after centuries of development of Chan Buddhism, to dramatically illustrate the essential iconoclastic flavor of Bodhidharma's (i.e. Chan's) teaching.

The legend further holds that Bodhidharma thought Wu Di did not have sufficient appreciation of the value of his teaching, so he left for Luoyang. The Emperor unsuccessfully sent emissaries to stop him after realizing too late the greatness of Bodhidharma's message. Bodhidharma took himself to Northern Wei by crossing the Yangtze River, according to one version, by standing on a reed. There were many handsome temples in Luoyang, and the study of Buddhist scriptures was carried out with great earnestness. By one account, it was "swanning" with monks vying with one another for fame as learned Buddhist scholars. Their common endeavor was to find salvation through reading and interpreting the sutras and sastras which had been brought from India. These scholastic monks were called *jiaojia* (scripture-family monks) and pursued what was then the orthodox path to enlightenment. While at Luoyang, Bodhidharma supposedly criticized the *jiaojia*'s mistaken approach:

> The scriptures are the finger that points to the moon of Enlightenment. When one can see the moon, there is no further use for the finger. But to become lost in the study and interpretation of the scriptures, in other words to forget to look at the moon, to forget about attaining Enlightenment, is to set Buddhism on its head. Both the Buddha and the common man have the true nature. To see this clearly, practice dhyana. When you arrive at the unshakable conviction that the "common man and the saint are one and the same," you will have no further need to follow after the written teachings of the scriptures (Awakawa, 1981: 64).

Stone gateway leading to what is reputed to be the cave where
Bodhidharma meditated facing a wall for nine years.
Photo courtesy of Steven Scherling.

After having said this, Bodhidharma found that he was an unwelcome stranger, slandered against, even hated and abused. He was forced to obtain his food by begging. He went to and ascended Mount Song (Songshan) where he practiced ascetic contemplation. One source states that it was then that he went to the monastery of *Shaolinsi* ("Young Forest Temple," Japanese: *Shorinji*) in Henan Province.* He was also not welcomed there, the head monk, by one account, throwing him out of the temple (Chow and Spangler, 1982: 10).

*As opposed to other "Shaolin" temples, particularly the Shaolin temple located in Fujian Province which also has been associated with the martial arts.

From his travels in China, Bodhidharma realized that because scholastic and philosophical Buddhism was dominant, Chinese Buddhists failed to grasp the reality of true Buddhism. Convinced that he must promulgate true Buddhism and aware that this could not be conveyed in lectures, he decided to demonstrate it with his body. Thus he took up his abode in a cave facing a high cliff, opposite the Shaolin Monastery and, according to the *Records*, meditated in silence before a wall for nine years.

Bodhidharma's "wall-gazing" meditation can be considered literally, that is, physically "sitting" or symbolically. At first blush, wall-gazing for nine years seems incredulous. However, it is something that, while astonishing, is apparently physically possible. One firsthand account from the middle of the last century, by a Reverend Joseph Edkins, confirms that a Chinese monk had been engaged in silently facing a wall for six years like Bodhidharma. Edkins stated that the monk "could read, but never took book in hand. His only employment was to mutter the prayers of his religion in a low voice." Edkins wrote a note and passed it to the monk. It said that the monk's vow not to speak was of no benefit. "The monk looked at the paper, read it, and gave a faint smile. He refused to write any reply . . ." (Welch, 1967: 323).

Bodhidharma lore states that Bodhidharma once fell asleep while in biguan at Shaolin. He was so penitent when he awoke that he punished himself by cutting off his eyelids so as to assure himself of no further hindrances with his meditation. Legend has it that on the spot where Bodhidharma let fall his eyelids, there grew an unfamiliar aromatic plant whose leaves were used by the eager neophytes to brew a drink which would keep them awake while they meditated. This was tea! However, the truth is that tea was not introduced into China until centuries later. Nonetheless, it is still part of the *cha-noyu* ceremony to drink tea before a "portrait" of Bodhidharma.

One of the reasons given for Bodhidharma's nine-year biguan is that he hoped he might find among the many monks who passed by, one who would qualify to succeed him. As the story is related in the *Records*, while Bodhidharma was engaged in "wall gazing," a well-known forty-year-old scholarly monk from Luoyang, named Shen Guang (487-593 C.E.), who was versed in both Daoism and Confucianism, came to hear of Bodhidharma. Shen Guang went to Shaolin to speak with him, but when Bodhidharma paid no attention, he went away. Three years later he returned, in mid-winter (the ninth of December), and he stayed all night in the snow. By morning he was covered up to his waist in drifts; yet he still stood there, intent upon asking Bodhidharma for the true teaching (Barnet and Burto, 1982: 30). Suzuki offers a possible version of Shen Guang's supplication:

> History gives examples of ancient truth-seekers, who are willing for the sake of enlightenment to have the marrow extracted from their bones, their blood spilled to feed the hungry, to cover the muddy road with their hair, or to throw themselves into the mouth of a hungry tiger. What am I? Am I not also able to give myself up upon the altar of truth?

Bodhidharma replied (in part):

> The incomparable teaching of Buddhism can be comprehended only after a long and hard discipline and by enduring what is most difficult to endure and by practicing what is most difficult to practice (Suzuki, 1978: 41).

Upon hearing Bodhidharma's reply Shen Guang was deeply moved, and in order to show his sincerity to be instructed, he took a sword or sharp knife, cut off his left arm, and presented it to Bodhidharma.

One scholar states that when Shen Guang's arm was cut off, Bodhidharma said to him, "Ah, you are earnest," and that such an act shows how serious one must be to be able to attain enlightenment (Kanazawa, 1979: 76). Hearing these words, Shen Guang experienced enlightenment. Bodhidharma appointed him to be his successor as the second Chinese patriarch of Chan Buddhism and changed his name to Hui Ke (Eka in Japanese).

Whether Hui Ke actually cut off his arm to prove his worthiness is open to speculation. A more believable account holds that his arm was cut off by robbers who had attacked him at the urging of the *jiaojia* (Barnet and Burto, 1982: 30). Even more probable is the theory that this self-amputation, like the encounter with Emperor Wu Di, is a creation of later Chan Buddhists. In this case, it is symbolic of Shen Hui's (670-762 C.E.) heretical (and losing) claim to the position of the Sixth Patriarchship (Hu Shih, 1953: 7-8). Hui Ke's cutting off of his arm should not be taken literally. One scholar states it was a symbolic act, the self-amputation being interpreted as "casting aside all traditional methods for arriving at the truth" (Ross, 1966: 60).

Close-up of the entrance to Bodhidarma's cave. Steles commemorate his associations with Buddhism. Photo courtesy of Steven Scherling

Biguan has another, and perhaps more likely, symbolic meaning. While it is not disputed that a specific physical method of sitting in meditation was a central part of Chinese Chan and later Japanese Zen Buddhists' activity, it should be differentiated from the doctrine of biguan meditation (*Hekkwan*, in Japanese). Even those who take Bodhidharma's biguan literally, give the patriarch some "time outs." Martial artist David Chow states that one should "not get the impression that Bodhidharma was staring at the rock wall for twenty-four hours a day. This, despite some fanciful Chan histories, is not true. . . . One account suggests that he meditated on the mound of leaves for two-hour periods at dawn and dusk with further contemplation inside his cave" (Chow and Spangler, 1982: 10). Symbolically, biguan refers to the sitter's inner state. It is more properly a metaphor for the form of sudden enlightenment which Chan proposed, rather than a literal definition of a meditation posture. As a contemporary martial artist and Zen student has stated:

"Wall" stands for a barrier which prevents the world's dust and corruption entering and for a shield which guards against all delusive ideas and sensuous images; "gazing" means to confront one's self in illuminating meditation, relying only on one's inner resources (Stevens, 1983, p. 82).

It was Suzuki's opinion that the teaching of the symbolic meaning of biguan, not his physically sitting in zazen, was what made Bodhidharma the first Chinese patriarch of Chan (Suzuki, 1978: 86).

Bodhidharma's Death and Other Legends

Most sources say Bodhidharma returned to India after the acceptance of Hui Ke as his disciple and successor. One popular version has it that a Chinese named Song Yun, a lay officer from Dunhuang of the Northern Wei Dynasty, was returning from a three-year pilgrimage to India, which had been ordered by Emperor Xiao Zhuang (reigned 528-530 C.E.). On the way he met Bodhidharma in the Cong Lin or "Onion Pass." Bodhidharma was on his way back to India, but he was wearing only one shoe (or as sometimes recounted, a sandal). As a source from 1307 C.E. states: "Carrying a shoe in his hand he went home quietly, without ceremony" (Suzuki, 1978: 253). Later, when hearing Song Yun's story, disciples opened Bodhidharma's gilded and lacquered cloth coffin, by one account at the Emperor's order, and found his body gone and only one shoe (or sandal) in the coffin (Chow and Spangler, 1982: 13).

Another version states that he traveled to Japan in the year 613 C.E. (sometimes coming from Korea), crossing the Sea of Japan, standing, variably on a reed, rush leaf or lotus leaf. Reconciling the various versions of the tradition produces interesting results. For example, if he was 110 before he came to China in 520 C.E. and it took three years to get there, he would have been 196 years old when he arrived in Japan. According to the *Nihon shoki* (720 C.E.), Daruma, in the form of a beggar, had a chance roadside encounter with the Prince Regent, Shotoku Taishi (593-622 C.E.), who, like Emperor Wu Di of China, also just happened to be a zealous champion of Buddhism. The prince spoke with the poor hungry man, who had very bright eyes, gave him food and drink, and even covered him with some of his own clothes. The next day, a retainer sent to look after the beggar found him dead. The prince was saddened to hear this and ordered that the beggar be buried on the spot where he was found. The prince later felt that this man was no ordinary man and after a few days had the grave inspected. It was discovered that the body was gone but that the prince's clothing was still in the coffin. This version from the *Nihon Shoki* does not identify the beggar as Daruma. However, a later account in the *Genkyo Shakuso* (1322 C.E.) makes a positive identification (McFarland, 1987: 17-18). Even today, in a small temple in Nara prefecture, one can be shown the exact site where Daruma is reportedly buried. This temple, which identifies Shotoku as its founder also has two large stones within its precinct which indicate the exact place where the prince and Daruma spoke. The Shotoku Taishi legend interesting parallels two bits of Chinese lore: the meeting with Emperor Wu Di and the disappearance of Bodhidharma's body.

Bodhidharma is also purported to have died in northern China, but as one might expect, this story too is shrouded in mystery. The year normally given for his death is 534 C.E., but one also finds references to the years 527, 529 and 540. Dao Xuan states that Bodhidharma died in Luoyang, but no details are given. It is often stated that Bodhidharma died of poison as a result of intrigue on the part of rival teachers. The murderous culprits are actually identified in one source, wherein it is also stated that they finally succeeded in poisoning Bodhidharma after no less than six unsuccessful attempts (Shaw, 1961: 107). They buried his body as quickly as possible. Alternatively Hui Ke supposedly buried Bodhidharma's body on the bank of the Ko (Huang) River. Yet another version says Bodhidharma is buried at the Pagoda of the Bear's Ear, at Mount Yu Li in northern China. Lastly, he supposedly lies at Xiung Er (Bear's Ear) Mountain in Henan Province.

Bodhidharma as the Father of Asian Martial Arts

In writing his thesis on Bodhidharma, the author reviewed hundreds of volumes of academic works, and in this genre only two scholars mentioned Bodhidharma's relationship to Chinese martial arts. Thus, one must look primarily to contemporary martial arts literature to find references to the nexus between the martial arts and Bodhidharma. Unfortunately, in the great majority of cases, contemporary martial arts authors simply parrot bits and pieces of the corpus of Buddhist material relating to the patriarch. More often than not, the historicity of Bodhidharma is taken without question, usually by a catchall sentence like the following: "Bodhidharma was the monk who brought Zen Buddhism from India to China in 520 C.E."

The martial arts tradition, however, adds activities to those which the *Biographies*, the *Records* and subsequent Buddhist literature attributed to Bodhidharma while he was at the Shaolin Temple. According to a mostly oral tradition, while at the Shaolin Temple, Bodhidharma initiated several programs which caused him to be considered the father of Asian martial arts. One martial arts author has said that "it can be asserted *with fair certainty* [italics added] that unarmed defense principles were advanced through Chan Buddhist religious practices during the sixth century. The holy man considered by most modern sources to be the father of the martial arts is Bodhidharma" (Chow and Spangler, 1982: 32). Others refer to Bodhidharma as the person who "invented" the martial arts. In Japan, Daruma is considered the "Patron Saint" of Japanese martial artists (Reid, 1984: 26) and his "portrait" hangs in most dojos.

The reason for such a venerable position in the martial arts is that Bodhidharma gave the monks at the Shaolin Temple something more than a new Buddhist perspective. The Shaolin Temple had the long-established purpose of being a nexus for Indian monks who came to China to translate Indian sutras into Chinese. It was built in 495 C.E. by the order of Emperor Xiao Wen of the Northern Wei Dynasty for an Indian monk and had a specially constructed platform for the Indian monks to use for translating.

At some point after Bodhidharma arrived at the temple (and perhaps after the self-amputation by Hui Ke, although this incident is rarely mentioned in the martial arts literature), student-monks became willing to undertake his dhyana brand of meditation. In order to properly perform his dhyana, a high degree of physical stamina was required. As the tradition goes, the monks were so weak that they would fall asleep during Bodhidharma's meditation lessons. He was forced to strengthen the monks before they could properly undertake dhyana meditation. In order to improve their "flaccid and emaciated bodies" he instituted a program of physical education including calisthenics, respiratory exercises, and, by some accounts, Indian fighting techniques. In the mid-1980's a western visitor to the Shaolin Temple was told by its 77-year old abbot, "Zen Buddhism and Kung Fu [*gongfu*] were born together, as two faces of the same coin, as two ways to reach the same goal: internal peace" (Terzani, 1987: 179). In 1982, another interested traveler also journeyed to the temple. He visited the training hall and an old monk who was guiding him pointed to the murals depicting martial arts practice and proffered the standard tradition:

> Master Da Mo, who lived 1,400 years ago, was the founder of Zen in Chinese Buddhism. His school... is called 'Wall Watching" ... as ... [his students] sat cross-legged meditating for a long time. They got fatigued and exhausted easily. To keep their bodies and minds free, the monks did a lot of exercises every day. In the course of time these exercises developed into the renowned Shaolin (*gongfu*) (Wu, 1982: 36).

Bodhidharma's emphasis was supposedly on the respiratory system for the cultivation of intrinsic bioenergy, called *qi* after Daoist nomenclature. In India this vital force had been known for centuries as *prajna* (or *prajna-vayu*). In Japan and Korea it became known as *ki*, and on Okinawa as *chii hara*. Bodhidharma's emphasis on qi is considered by some to have been his main contribution. It is simply assumed that since Bodhidharma was a member of the kshatriya caste he automatically knew yogic breathing and other martial exercises and techniques. In order to strengthen the Shaolin monks' bodies so that they could meditate "he taught them breathing techniques and exercises that are thought to have been the basis of the modern martial arts" (Reid, 1984: 61). The famous *sanchin* breathing kata, incorporated in over a dozen Okinawan karate styles is often attributed to Bodhidharma and has even been called the "lifework of Bodhidharma" (Russell, 1976: 76). Interestingly, according to Uechiryu style, the goal of sanchin is nothing less than enlightenment: "when thought processes are not necessary to perform an action"; in essence, the kata is repeated over and over until the performer does not have to think. The very essence of Zen!

Another purported martial arts creation of Bodhidharma is the "horse-riding stance," *qi ma bu* (*kee ma jaseh*, in Korean; *kiba dachi*, in Japanese), which was both a physical exercise as well as a meditation exercise. This stance is familiar to students of all Asian karate systems. The monks would be expected to remain in the horse-riding stance, without moving, for the length of time it took a stick of incense to burn, about one hour! This would be the only exercise that trainees would be taught for six months to a year (Rihner, 1978: 5). In the horse-riding stance, the monks practiced concentrating on one particular thought. They had to learn to conquer the pain from standing in this position for extended periods of time so as to make their minds as well as their bodies strong enough to endure. The horse-riding stance is sometimes called one of "Bodhidharma's Treasures" (Chow and Spangler, 1982: 12).

Disciplines and exercises which Bodhidharma taught for the health, vitality and spiritual development of the Shaolin monks were initially transmitted orally and later transcribed into written form. However, it has been estimated that these books of exercises were not written until a thousand years later (Reid, 1984: 27). They are known as the *Yijinjing* or the "Muscle Change Classic", the *Xisuijing* or "Marrow Cleansing Classic," and the *Shiba Luohan Shou* or the "Eighteen Hand Movements of the Luohan."

According to qigong tradition, the *Muscle Change Classic* was what taught the monks to change their physical weakness to strength. When these methods were integrated into martial arts training, it purportedly was found that the effectiveness and strength of the practitioners' techniques were greatly improved. The *Muscle Change Classic*, as it exists today, consists of two parts, the first relating to *waidan*, or external qigong exercises, and the second part containing *neidan*, or internal qigong exercises. In the former, the practitioner develops the muscles of his limbs while in the latter he perfects such techniques as abdominal breathing in order to build up qi in the lower *dantian*. Neidan builds up the torso and internal parts of the body, but not the limbs.

Once all the regimens of the *Muscle Change Classic* were mastered, those of the *Marrow Washing Classic* were undertaken. These taught the proper use of qi to clean the bone marrow and strengthen the blood and immune system, while at the same time energizing the brain so as to attain enlightenment. Because this classic was much more difficult to understand and practice than the *Muscle Change Classic*, its training methods were only secretly transmitted to very few disciples in each generation. According to one authority, the *Marrow Washing Classic* has only been revealed to the public in the last twenty years. One professor of Asian history states the commonly held tradition that Bodhidharma "taught the monks a style of boxing for self-defense as well as for reinvigorating the body after a period of meditation. In this manner arose the Shaolin style of boxing which became famous in later Chinese history" as Shaolin quanfa. This martial arts system primarily uses waidan martial qigong, while internal styles such as taijiquan, baguaquan and xingiquan developed from neidan methods. Hence, the internal/external dichotomy of martial arts' systems can be attributed to writings which are in turn attributed to Bodhidharma.

One martial arts author suggests that the wisdom contained in these classics, not searching for enlightenment, was the real cause of his biguan, postulating that Bodhidharma: "*pondered* [italics added] nine years on how to solve the 'weak and sickly' condition of the Shaolin monks, and that when he emerged, he wrote two classics, the *Muscle and Tendon Classic* and the *Marrow Washing Classic*" (Yang, 1989: 67).

So, depending upon which martial arts author one reads or which tradition one follows, one can hear almost limitless varieties of what Bodhidharma accomplished as well as when, how, and why he did so. Recollecting the scant historically reliable evidence of either his existence, his actual teaching of Chan principles, or anything which proves Bodhidharma's relationship to the martial arts in general or specifically to the two classics and the eighteen Luohan system of exercises, one is hard put to connect him definitively to any martial arts tradition. Furthermore, there are no extant writings even remotely contemporary with Bodhidharma's purported life-span which buttress the claims found in martial arts literature.

Essentially everything that is today passed on in Asian martial arts traditions is a product of later oral and written traditions, including stories related by later martial arts teachers who, like their Chan compatriots, respectfully attribute sage teachings and miraculous actions to Bodhidharma. One example of such traditions is that Bodhidharma was "killing two birds with one stone" by teaching Indian breathing and fighting techniques along with Chan dhyana meditative practices. Another commonly held, but unsubstantiated belief, is that the patriarch did not introduce new exercises or techniques, but rather introduced *wude* (martial virtue) to an undisciplined and unruly martial arts community:

> Prior to the arrival of Ta-Mo [Da Mo] Chinese martial artists trained primarily to fight and were fond of bullying weaker folk. Ta-Mo [Da Mo] brought wu-te [wude], which taught that the marital arts are really meant to promote spiritual development and health, not fighting (Reid, 1984: 27).

Chinese Shaolin styles are not the only ones which trace themselves back to Bodhidharma. Earlier this century a Japanese named Doshin-so traveled to the monastery and after studying the murals depicting the Indian fighting techniques brought back with him what is known as Shorinji Kempo. This Japanese style has been described as a combination of religion, martial arts and Zen meditation and in Japan is officially registered as a religion, Kongo-Zen (Fox, 1983: 76).

One of the greatest martial arts practioners and theorists of the twentieth century, Funakoshi Gichin, who is responsible for the introduction and popularizing of Okinawan karate in Japan, stated unequivocally that the founder of Shorinji-kempo was Bodhidharma (Funakoshi, 1984: 36). As of the mid-1980's Shorinji Kempo was taught in seventeen countries, with Japan having over 2,500 chapters with nearly a million members. All of this martial art activity is inferentially traceable to Bodhidharma. Further, Shorinji-kempo is but one of a dozen styles in Japan that claims ancestral roots to Bodhidharma's Shaolin "style" (Corcoran, 1983: 72). Thus, in addition to Zen, there are at least one million adherents to a martial tradition which Bodhidharma is credited with creating over fourteen centuries ago.

Bodhidharma's Shaolin recipe contained several other ingredients which were common throughout the years to both Zen Buddhism and oriental fighting arts. Quite important is the tradition of the master-disciple relationship, as seen in the relationship between Bodhidharma and Hui Ke, whereby knowledge is transmitted person to person. As Ueshiba Kisshomaru states, this transmission is considered to be an "endless circle of student and master . . . [giving] both the teacher and the taught the feeling of being part of a continuum of learning" (Ueshiba, 1984: 85). Thus, the martial arts instructor is much like the Chan or Zen *roshi*; both act as personal guides to the students in mastering the difficulties of their respective tasks. In this regard, it is interesting to note that the place where the guide transmits his knowledge to the disciple, whether *dojang* or *dojo*, means "Place of Enlightenment." These words are derived from the Sanskrit word *bodhimanda* (or *bodhimandala*), a place devoted to religious exercises "where self undergoes transformation into the egoless self." This focus is directly related to not only Buddhism in general, but Chan in particular, and therefore Bodhidharma.

One tradition rarely mentioned is the Patriarch's connection with the Triads, or as they have been roughly described, the Chinese Mafia. While "secret societies" in China go back over a thousand years, the true historical beginnings of the Triads occurred during the reign of the third Qing emperor, Yong Zheng (r. 1722-35 C.E.). The seminal event in Triad tradition was the destruction of the Fujian Shaolin Temple by imperial order. The Qing Empire was ruled by Manchus, whom the Chinese considered foreigners. Many secret societies were formed or revitalized to encourage Chinese nationalism and patriotism under the motto "Overthrow the Qing and restore the Ming." Because the

Shaolin monks were accomplished warriors, martial artists and strategists, the Emperor considered them a threat and thus ordered the temple destroyed. Regarding this event, not surprisingly, Triad authorities state that "there is little basis in historical fact" (Booth, 1991: 9).

Nonetheless, to this very day, the triad societies have, like Zen Buddhists and Asian martial artists, seen value in incorporating part of the Bodhidharma legend into their traditions. According to Triad lore, when the imperial forces burned out the monastery, only eighteen monks escaped alive. Of these, thirteen soon died, leaving the "First Five Ancestors" of the Triads. In order to escape the Qing forces who were still after them, they had to find a way to get across a wide river. A grass sandal which had been brought with them from the temple, magically turned into a boat, allowing them to cross the river. The grass slipper, of course, was supposedly Bodhidharma's. One is tempted to conclude that this may have been the sandal said to have been missing from or found in Bodhidharma's coffin. Triad tradition says, however, that in a battle subsequent to the river crossing both "precious grass sandals" were lost.

However, the symbolic value of Bodhidharma's sandals was not lost. In Triad lodges there is an altar upon which is placed a large red wooden tub. This tub holds all the "precious objects" of the society, including a grass sandal. "It represents one of a magic pair of sandals belonging to *Tat Mo* [Damo], the deity of *Siu Lam* [Shaolin] Monastery. Tat Mo is actually the Chinese name for Bodhidharma..." (Booth, 1991: 180-186). It should also be mentioned that, even today in Hong Kong and Taiwan, martial arts are sometimes connected with the Triads.

Conclusion

Unraveling the hoary lore and traditions surrounding Bodhidharma is an impossible task. There are essentially three major questions: 1) whether a Bodhidharma existed at all and, if he did, what his relationship was, if any, with 2) Chan Buddhism, and 3) Shaolin quanfa and thereby most Asian martial arts.

According to a basically pessimistic interpretation of the literature, there never was an historical Bodhidharma and thus all accounts of Bodhidharma, whether relating to Chan Buddhism or martial arts, are purely legendary. Furthermore, Bodhidharma was a fabricated personage created long after his purported life by later Chan Buddhists, most likely at the time of the sixth Chinese Patriarch Hui Neng (638-713 C.E.), who is generally regarded as the person under whom true Chan Buddhism began in China. It follows that there was a real usefulness in custom-designing a "First Chinese Patriarch." A direct succession from the Buddha himself, through an unbroken line of twenty-eight Indian patriarchs and then six Chinese patriarchs (first promulgated in the *Records*), would add considerably to the prestige of the nascent Chan sect. From the perspective of these later Chanists, one asks what characteristics and qualities would they have wanted the ideal candidate to possess in order to bridge the gap between the Buddha and Chinese Chan? First, the individual would have to have been an Indian, thereby providing a direct connection with both India and, through the posthumously created line of patriarchs, the Buddha himself. Second, who could refute a "mind-to-mind" unwritten or even nonverbal transmission from the Buddha to Kashyapa, his disciple, through twenty-five other Indian patriarchs to Prajnatara, Bodhidharma, Hui Ke and ultimately to Hui Neng. Even the first mention of the "flower sermon," whereby the Buddha transmitted mind-to-mind to Kashapa, appeared only in 1036 C.E.

Third, if Bodhidharma were a later creation, he could not have left anything in writing in the sixth century. Therefore, the later Chanists had a blank slate which they could fill with utterances containing fully developed Chan perspective and attribute them back to the first Chinese patriarch. Later Chan Buddhists could not choose an historical Indian monk like Kumarajiva who played a central role in bringing Buddhism to China by translating important sutras because, being historical, his deeds and thoughts were known and would not include the distinctive flavor of later Chan. Conversely, several important Chinese Buddhists who did in fact propagate core elements of what would later become Chan Buddhism, such as Seng Zhao (or Seng Chao, 384-416 C.E.) and Dao Sheng (360-434 C.E.), might have fit the bill, except they were not Indian.

Likewise, in tracing their respective roots back to Bodhidharma, martial artists found utility, credibility and the endorsement which a thousand-year-old tradition brings to any style or art. This process was made all the easier by the later Chan Buddhists "adopting" Bodhidharma. Chinese martial artists merely "piggybacked" on the widespread Chan reverence for the Patriarch and simply added the *Muscle Change Classic, Marrow Cleansing Classic* and the *Eighteen Luohan* to the other legacies of Bodhidharma. There are those who have even suggested that Bodhidharma's name was a later amalgamation, "*bodhi,*" meaning intuitive wisdom and knowledge, being coupled with "*dharma,*" meaning the law by which all things in the world are governed and controlled in accordance with Buddhist principles.

A more realistic perspective holds that there is a kernel of truth in the Bodhidharma tradition, that there was in fact an historical person who was an Indian monk who did travel to China early in the sixth century. The reference to Sraana Bodhidharma in the *Luoyang* is probably to a different Bodhidharma. However, the reference to an Indian Buddhist meditating monk who practiced Mahayana Buddhism in the *Biographies* is sufficient for this writer to accept the proposition that there was probably a Bodhidharma and that it was this Bodhidharma who was chosen by later Chan Buddhists to wear a patriarch's mantle woven out of later-created cloth. But much of its fabric was fabricated. One of the circumstances indicating that the above legend may be true is that the Buddhist emperor De Zong gave his imprimatur to the true teachings of Chan as well as settling the controversies regarding Chan patriarchal lineage in 768 C.E. and thereby establishing Bodhidharma as a historical figure. One historian has stated Bodhidharma "had comparatively little importance to his contemporaries. It was only with the growing importance of the Chan sect (8th-11th centuries C.E.) that Bodhidharma grew in stature as the twenty-eighth Indian patriarch and first Chinese patriarch and founder of the Chan sect in China" (Chapin, 1945-46: 74).

Concomitantly, with regard to Asian martial arts, an argument can be made that Bodhidharma was also later "adopted" by them, in part as a result of the connections which developed between them and Chan and Zen Buddhism. Chan Buddhists had as one of their main Bodhidharma stories his nine-year biguan at the Shaolin Temple, which had come to be famous as a martial arts center. All China knew the fighting prowess exercised by the Shaolin monks in assisting Emperor Tai Zong maintain his reign during the Tang Dynasty (Reid, 1984: 61). Essentially, the Shaolin Temple is connected with great quanfa monks, and Bodhidharma was connected with the Shaolin Temple. In the 1500's, when it is speculated that the *Muscle Change Classic*, the *Marrow Cleansing Classic* and the *Eighteen Hand Movements of the Luohan* were written, it is probable that Chinese martial artists merely copied earlier Chan Buddhists by attributing these books to an ancient master. Who better than Bodhidharma, who, it could be claimed, had brought breathing and fighting secrets from India?

The author has an additional theory regarding Bodhidharma's connection with the Asian martial arts: he is the paradigm of will power, self-discipline and determination, the mentor of "long and hard discipline and . . . enduring what is most difficult to do and . . . practicing what is most difficult to practice." Whether true or not, the tales relating to Bodhidharma ascribe to him the single most important virtue required to both (1) attain enlightenment as well as (2) reach the highest levels of Asian martial arts proficiency. Life and death conflicts on a personal, man-to-man basis were considered probable for a martial artist until relatively recent times in Asia, and such determination, self-discipline and dedication were a *sine qua non* just to survive. This same determination, akin to willingly having the marrow extracted from one's bones, was also necessary to reach enlightenment through Chan and Zen meditation. Thus, ever since the time of Bodhidharma, the paradigm for successfully mastering both Chan Buddhism *and* Asian martial arts was the same: an almost super-human determination and self-discipline to conquer the body and control the mind so as to attain enlightenment in the former and either victory or the ready acceptance of death in the latter.

Bodhidharma was the personification of this paradigm in many respects. As Shotokan master Nishiyama Hidetaka has stated with regard to Bodhidharma's arduous overland trek from India to China, it was "no mean feat and testifies to Dharuma's [Daruma's] powers of physical and mental endurance" (Nishiyama, 1950: 16). More importantly, however, was Bodhidharma's nine-year biguan at the Shaolin Temple. Nothing better exemplifies the sheer determination to conquer one's self. The feat, apocryphal or not, has always been glorified for the depth of its commitment. It has been said that during his biguan his concentration was so great that he could hear the screaming of ants; his gaze bore a hole through the cave wall; and his determination not to interrupt his concentration was so strong that, in addition to Bodhidharma tearing off his eyelids, his legs atrophied and fell off (giving rise to the legless daruma dolls of Japan).

Bodhidharma has always been the personification of the fierce inner strength and spiritual determination it takes to reach enlightenment. Over the years this determination has been equated by Zen and Chan masters to the determination of a drowning man to get air. Such selfless determination mirrors that of the Buddha himself, who supposedly made a solemn vow that "though his bones wasted away and his blood dried up, he would not leave his seat" in meditation under the pipal tree until he reached enlightenment (Basham, 1959: 258).

Bodhidharma has always been one of the most favored subjects of Chan and Zen artists, and interesting and unusual canons of representation regarding him have developed over the centuries. Early paintings of Bodhidharma (the earliest dates from 1054 C.E., just after the *Records*) depict him as a serene and passive individual, not unlike how a "holyman" would be represented in Western religious or secular art. However, over time, Bodhidharma was iconographically transformed so that he is now almost always depicted with a frightening, stern or ferocious demeanor, with fiery eyes and other features which are intended to communicate intense determination. However, what has intrigued this writer in reviewing hundreds of paintings and reproductions of paintings, sculptures, ceramics, dolls, etc., of Bodhidharma in numerous positions and postures, is that never once was there a single representation of Bodhidharma which in any manner, shape or form could resemble the horse-riding stance or any other martial arts position, kata, hyung, or exercise, even those from the *Eighteen Hand Movements of the Luohan!**

*Conversely, in Japan Daruma has become associated with everything from dolls to toys, kites, games, snowmen, folk holidays, political elections and festivals, and he has been represented in numerous forms including a woman, a prostitute, and a transvestite (McFarland, passim).

Not only do later paintings confirm this iconological transition, but so do carved steles at the Shaolin Temple itself. Surrounding the main building of the temple are several such upright stone monuments, rubbings from which provide a valuable sequence of images of Bodhidharma. Scholars investigating these rubbings have found that, in accordance with their dating, Bodhidharma's foreignness and strangeness became more and more emphasized over time, and his expression became increasingly forbidding and dour. They discovered that "from Yuan times on an increasingly grotesque foreign type of Bodhidharma image came into fashion" (Bush and Mair, 1977-78: 42). In fact, the researchers in their study state that several of the later artistic recreations show pugnacious facial characterizations that "somehow seem in keeping with the Shaolin Temple's promotion of the arts of boxing and cudgeling" (Bush and Mair, 1977-78: 47). Thus, as time went by not only was the story of the life of Bodhidharma molded to fit the needs of later Chan Buddhists and Chinese martial arts traditions, but the pictorial representations of the Patriarch were also modified to inspire the viewer to seek to achieve the ultimate in self-discipline, whether for Buddhist or martial arts purposes.

Painting of Bodhidharma rendered by Michael Spiessbach.
It follows an original by Niten (Miamoto Musashi).

In the end, at least from a martial arts perspective, a twentieth century Western martial artist is faced with a choice which reflects the classic tension between the cerebral and visceral imperatives in all of us. There is no definitive body of proof confirming or denying Bodhidharma's existence, much less his accomplishments. However, what does exist is a martial arts tradition which goes back centuries, if not over a millennium. Most martial artists choose to accept the Bodhidharma tradition because he who accepts it becomes part of its ancient, esoteric and arcane legacy. Until proof is unearthed that Bodhidharma either did not exist and/or had no connection with the martial arts, contemporary martial artists, particularly Occidentals, will surely continue to opt to be part of a time-honored martial arts Way which can claim fifteen hundred years of development. Human nature, Western or Asian, this author feels, will usually lean toward this choice, notwithstanding the lack of empirical data regarding the historicity of someone whom they *want to believe in*. Thus, the legends and "make believe" regarding Bodhidharma, whether Chan or martial arts related, will continue for the same psychological reasons legends of countless other holy men exist, characters of inspiration or personifications of paradigm virtues. In this regard, the conclusions scholars have reached with regard to the Buddha apply equally to Bodhidharma:

> The strongest lines in his character and personality come, not from the certainties of established fact, but from the imaginative power of human beings which love to dower the great with the wealth of its own image-making faculties. The great man is so often better known to us by what he never said or did, but by what people believed he said or did (Ludowyk, 1958: 38).

REFERENCES

AWAKAWA, Y. (1981). *Zen painting*. Tokyo: Kodansha International.

BASHAM, H. (1959). *The wonder that was India*. New York: Grove Press.

BARNET, S., AND BURTO, W. (1982). *Zen ink paintings*. Tokyo: Kodansha International.

BOOTH, M. (1991). *The Triads*. New York: St. Martin's Press.

BUSH, S. AND MAIR, V. (1977-78). Some Buddhist portraits and images of the Lu and Ch'an sects in tenth and thirteenth century China. *Archives of Asian Art*, pp. 32- 51.

CHANG, C. (1969). *Original teachings of Ch'an Buddhism: Selected from "The transmission of the lamp."* New York: Pantheon Press.

CHAPIN, H. (1945-46). Three early portraits of Bodhidharma. *Archives of the Chinese Art Society of America*, pp. 66-97.

CHEN, K. (1964). *Buddhism in China*. Princeton: Princeton University Press.

CHOW, D., AND SPRANGLER, R. (1982). *Kung-fu history, philosophy and technique*. Burbank: Unique Publications.

CORCORAN, J., AND FARKAS, E. (1983). *Martial arts: Tradition, history, people*. New York: Gallery Publications.

Dumoulin, H. (1963). *A history of Zen Buddhism*. New York: Pantheon Press.

FOX, M. (1983, February). The dharma of Shorinji Kempo. *Black Belt*, pp. 76-79.

FUNAKOSHI, G. (1984). *Karate-do: My way of life*. Tokyo: Kodansha International.

HAKUYU, T., AND GLASSMAN, B. (1976). *On Zen practice*. Los Angeles: Zen Center of Los Angeles.

HOOVER, T. (1978). *Zen Culture*. London: Routledge and Kegan Paul, Ltd.

HU, SHIH. (1953, April). Ch'an (Zen) Buddhism in China, its history and development. *Philosophy East and West*, pp. 3-24.

KANAZAWA, H. (1979). *Japanese ink paintings: Early Zen masterpieces*. Tokyo: Kodansha International.

LANCIOTTI, L. (1949). New historic contributions to the person of Bodhidharma. *Artibus Asiae*, 12, 141-144.

LUDOWYK, E. (1958). *The footprints of the Buddha*. London: Allen and Unwin.

MATTSON, G. (1974). *Uechiryu karate do*. Plymouth: Peabody Publishing.

MCFARLAND, H. NEILL. (1987). *Daruma – the founder of Zen in Japanese art and popular culture*. Tokyo and New York: Kodansha International.

MIZUNO, K. (1982). *Buddhist sutras: Origin, development, transmission*.

Tokyo: Kosei Publishing Co.

NISHIYAMA, H., AND BROWN, R. (1950). *Karate: The art of empty hand fighting*. Rutland: Charles E. Tuttle and Co.

REID, H., AND CROUCHER, M. (1984). *The way of the warrior: The paradox of the martial arts*. London: Century Publishing Co.

RIBNER, S. AND CHIN, R. (1978). *The martial arts*. New York: Harper and Row.

ROSS, N. (1966). *Three ways of Asian wisdom*. New York: Simon and Schuster.

RUSSELL, W. (1976). *Karate: The energy connection*. New York: Delacorte Press.

SEKIDA, K. (1983). *Zen training: Methods and philosophy*. Tokyo: John Weatherhill.

SHAW, R. (Trans.). (1961). *Hekigan roku* [The blue cliff records]. London: Michael Joseph Ltd.

STEVENS, J. (Trans.). (1983). *Zenga*. London: Routledge and Kegan Paul Ltd.

SUZUKI, D. (1978). *Essays in Zen Buddhism: First series*. New York: Evergreen Press.

SUZUKI, D. (1969). *The Zen doctrine of no mind*. London: Rider and Co.

SUZUKI, D. (1971). *Zen and Japanese culture*. Princeton: Princeton University Press.

SUZUKI, D. (1982). *Living by Zen*. London: Rider and Company.

TERZANI, T. (1987). Behind the forbidden door. *China Inside and Out, Asia 2000* (Hong Kong ed.), pp. 176-188.

UESHIBA, K. *(1984). The spirit of aikido.* Tokyo: Kodansha International.

YANG, J. (1989). *The root of Chinese chigung*. Jamaica Plains: Yang Martial Art Association.

WELCH, H. (1967). *The practice of Chinese Buddhism 1900-1950*. Cambridge: Harvard University Press.

WU, J. (1982). Kung fu. *China Sights and Insights*, 2.

chapter 2

The Daoist Origins of the Chinese Martial Arts
by Charles Holcombe, Ph.D.

Daoist longevity exercises have greatly influenced China's martial art traditions. Here, an elderly gentleman stolls atop the Badaling section of the Great Wall. Long beards and the Long Wall are two of the many symbols for long life. Photos by M. DeMarco.

Some three decades ago Joseph Needham offered his opinion that "Chinese boxing . . . probably originated as a department of Taoist [Daoist] physical exercises."[1] This arresting hypothesis manages to strike us as both strange and yet oddly comfortable at the same time. We would expect that religion should have little to do with the deadly business of combat; yet, to anyone even remotely acquainted with the Chinese martial arts, the Daoist imprint is unmistakable. The present chapter is intended to explore the implications of this Daoist paternity. What exactly does it mean to say that the martial arts began with Daoist exercises, and what does that then tell us about the martial arts?

To begin with, it goes without saying that we do not intend to imply that the specific forms of the modern martial arts necessarily derive from older Daoist practices. What we do mean is simply that the basic philosophical underpinnings of the Chinese martial arts are Daoist. Beyond this, I venture to suggest that a technique which is central to the modern martial arts actually originated in Daoism. This technique is what has relatively recently come to be labeled qigong—*qi*, meaning breath or air, and *gong*, meaning achievement. The art has been defined by a contemporary Chinese scholar as "an active process of physical and mental discipline through the training of the heart/mind, the training of breathing, the training of the body and other means, which takes as its main goal the strengthening of human physical co-ordination."[2] In other words, it is the bending of qi to human intentions or "Daoist breath control."

Qigong has been surprisingly pervasive in Chinese thought. Even staid Confucians advocated its practice. Mencius (c. 372-279 B.C.E.), for example, spoke of "cultivating my overwhelming qi," and in the twelfth century Zhu Xi (1130-1200) advocated the use of qigong breath control in his program of Neo-Confucian self-cultivation.[3] It is with the Daoist school, however, that the manipulation of the inner energies released by breath control is most intimately associated, and it was the Daoists who made the most extravagant claims for that technique. As the distinguished British Sinologist Arthur Waley put it, he who mastered Daoist breath control could "cure every disease, expose himself with immunity to epidemics, charm snakes and tigers, stop wounds from bleeding, stay under the water or walk upon it, stop hunger and thirst, and increase his own life-span."[4]

Such claims are fantastic. That they were, and sometimes still are, taken seriously can only be understood in the light of the Chinese scientific paradigm which took shape in the great eclectic *weltanschauung* of the Han dynasty (202 B.C.E.-220 C.E.). This Han world-view envisioned the universe to be, in Derk Bodde's words, "a harmoniously functioning organism," the actions of whose component parts were each mutually related.[5] The complex interactions of yin and yang and five basic elements (*wuxing*) produced the manifold phenomena of nature. Elaborate sets of correlations were then devised for each element, and it was assumed that the correlates reacted sympathetically to each other.

This view is nicely illustrated in the following passage from the second century C.E. Daoist classic *Taipingjing*:

> The nature of wood [one of the five elements] is humanity. If you contemplate humanity, therefore, you will be transported to the East, since the East is the master of humanity. The five directions [including the center] are all like this. The affairs of the world all follow their own kind. Therefore, if emperors and kings think peacefully, their governments will be peaceful as well, through the appeal of likeness.[6]

Viewed through the lenses of "modern science," it is easy to dismiss the logical process in operation here as "thought magic," in Murakami Yoshimi's words, and rationalize its continued acceptance in otherwise sophisticated Imperial China as an anachronistic relic of more primitive times.[7] In fact, however, this was not "magic" as Sir James Frazer might have defined it, but a mechanical tool for eliciting action at a distance through direct cause and effect, by means of the correlations among the five elements, and physical contact through the universal environment of qi.

Somewhat like the Western concept of the ether, qi was believed to be the substance surrounding and including all things, which brought even distant points into direct physical contact.[8] As the *Liezi* observed perhaps shortly after the fall of Han, "Heaven is merely amassed qi . . . When you bend, stretch, or breath, you are always moving inside Heaven."[9]

Since one single substance joined all corners of the cosmos into a single organic unity, it followed that mastery of qi was equivalent to mastery of the material universe. The key was the mind. "What man can imagine, he can always bring about," says the *Taipingjing*. "The mind and ideas are the pivotal mechanism of heaven and earth, and cannot be carelessly moved. If you cause harmonious ch'i [qi] to become disordered, calamities will occur daily."[10] It was seriously supposed that the words and actions of a properly cultivated gentleman could affect "places thousands of miles away," and in early imperial China, at least, such beliefs were not limited to so-called Daoists, but were shared by even such stolid Confucians as Fu Xuan (217-278), who pontificated that "the mind . . . is the controller of all things."[11]

The Han dynasty theoreticians were principally concerned about the implications of this discovery for government. It was supposed that the true ruler need only approach his task with a cultivated mind and settled heart for all the affairs of his domain to proceed in satisfactory harmony. But the ability of internal cultivation to transform external physical reality also had private significance, which in the long run proved to be of the greatest interest to most people. Specifically, proper circulation of qi could prolong one's life—perhaps indefinitely—and could enable the individual to accomplish otherwise incredible feats.

Nanjing Provincial Museum—a 2,000 year old jade burial suit made of nearly 2,600 squares of green jade. Such "jade cases" were only made for emperors and high-ranking aristocrats. Jade was often utilized in the making of weapons and clothing. Today, it remains a precious stone partly because it is associated with life-prolonging attributes.

The technique of manipulating qi for personal satisfaction can be traced back at least as far as the late fifth century B.C.E., when it was referred to as "moving qi" (*xing-qi*) on a jade pendant discovered recently by archaeologists.[12] The practice was evidently quite widespread even before the maturation of its theoretical explanation in the Han dynasty. According to the third century B.C.E. Daoist classic *Zhuangzi*:

> Huffing and puffing, exhaling the old and inhaling the new, the bear pull and the bird stretch, is for long life and only that. This is what the gentlemen of Taoist [Daoist] exercises, men who nourish their bodies, and those who study the long life of P'eng Tsu [the "Chinese Methuselah"] like.[13]

By the Han dynasty the therapeutic physical exercises—Zhuangzi's "bear pull and bird stretch"—were called *daoyin*. Excellent illustrations of these daoyin exercises dating from the early Han were found in 1973 on silk scrolls unearthed at the tomb complex at Mawangdui.[14] The purpose of these exercises was to loosen up the circulatory system to permit the free passage of qi. As the first century C.E. skeptic

Wang Chong wrote, Daoists "... suppose that if you do not shake, bend, and stretch the arteries in your body they will block up and not circulate, and if they do not circulate the accumulation will cause illness and death."[15]

Daoyin physical exercises were intended to facilitate the circulation of qi and were consequently secondary in importance to the actual manipulation of qi itself, which is often rendered in English as "breath control." This English term encompasses Zhuangzi's "huffing and puffing" without any problem but otherwise does not begin to do justice to the full range of the Chinese concept, since qi is not only breath but the very substance of the universe. Internally, within the human body, qi was envisioned as energy, often in fluid form.[16] When taken literally, as Daoist adepts so often did, this could be understood to mean saliva or the bodily fluids. According to one delightfully mystical text:

> The pure waters of the "jade pond" water the roots of the soul. If you investigate this and are able to cultivate it you can exist eternally. It is called "feeding upon nature." That which is natural is the "glorious pond." The "glorious pond" [refers to] the saliva in one's mouth. If you breathe in accordance with the rules and swallow it, you will not experience hunger.[17]

Details of the jade burial suit on display
in the Nanjing Provincial Museum.

Such technologies were understood as ways to physically recycle, conserve, and nourish the bodily qi which the therapeutic daoyin exercises had cleared passages for. A late Han dynasty adept named Wang Chen, for example, "practiced shutting off his qi and swallowing it, calling it embryonic breathing, and swallowing [the fluid] coughed up from the spring beneath his tongue, calling it embryonic feeding."[18]

These early qigong practices may have focused on actual respiration or the circulation of bodily fluids, but mental concentration must have been a necessary concomitant of "breath control" from its inception. With time the role of the mind came to loom even larger. In fully evolved qigong practice the energy of qi is channeled through the body under mental impulse.[19] It was this mental activity, developed into a form of meditation known as "holding on to the one" (*shouyi*) or "fixed thought" (*cunsi*), which actually unleashed the incredible powers of Daoist "breath control" noted by Arthur Waley.[20] Merely by thinking about it the adept can travel vast distances or cure diseases. As the *Baopuzi* recorded in the fourth century, "if you imagine the ch'i [qi] from your five internal organs emerging from your two eyes to surround your body like mist, . . . you can then share a bed with the victim of a plague [without danger]."[21]

The arrival of Indian Buddhism in China shortly after the birth of Christ may have added a new current to the stream of Chinese meditative practice but probably did little more than refine an already existing Daoist tradition.[22] The Parthian monk An Shihgao, for example, translated a Buddhist sutra on meditation through concentration on breathing (*anapana*) shortly after his arrival at the Han capital in 148 C.E., but by that time concentrated thought was also a central fixture of the Daoist tradition as well.[23] The meditative aspect of qigong should, therefore, be considered essentially as part of the main Daoist line of transmission, even while acknowledging the possibility that there were important Buddhist contributions.[24]

The meditative aspect of Daoist qigong in the Han dynasty is nicely illustrated by the following passage from the *Pengzujing*:

> Whoever moves his qi with the desire of eradicating the "hundred diseases" concentrates on wherever they are located. If his head aches he concentrates on his head, if his foot hurts he concentrates on his foot, combining his qi and sending it to attack it. In the time [the qi] takes to get there [the ache] will have dissipated by itself.[25]

Thus, although the term qigong had not yet been coined, qigong techniques were fully developed by the end of the Han dynasty. At the same time, true Daoist religion also emerged in the last century of the Han, and it soon absorbed and engulfed qigong. The new religion may have had distant precursors in shamanism, but its immediate ancestors are to be found among the *fangshi* ("gentlemen with prescriptions") who began to promote secret arts leading to immortality around the third century B.C.E.[26] Over the course of the next few centuries these arts evolved and spread until in the second century C.E. a man named Zhang Daoling (fl. c. 142) instigated a "religious revolution" by organizing a Daoist church dedicated to the pursuit of immortality.[27]

Simplicity Embracing Monastery located on a hill overlooking West Lake in Hangzhou City. It is noted as the place where Daoist Ge Hong alchemically prepared elixirs for attaining immortality.

After a rather conventional beginning studying the classics, the story goes, Zhang had retired to a mountain in modern-day Sichuan to "study the Dao of long life."[28] With divine direction he obtained a sacred text which enabled him to fly and work various other miracles.[29] Because of his new ability to cure disease, "the common people thronged to him and served him as their teacher, the households of his disciples reaching the tens of thousands."[30]

The new faith struck a responsive chord in late Han China, and the quest for immortality soon became all the rage among the elite. In the second century the *Taipingjing* claimed, perhaps with some hyperbole, that "the perfect gentlemen of the empire eschew office for immortality."[31] After the fall of Han, Chi Yin (313-384)—who strolled about with friends, "settled his heart, stopped eating grain, and cultivated the [Daoist] arts of Huang-Lao [the Yellow Emperor and Laozi]"—was typical of the lofty literati who dominated the era of division that followed.[32] Even Buddhism flourished in the immediate post-Han era largely "as a religion of immortal recipes."[33]

The medieval immortality cult was eclectic and borrowed from every conceivable tradition, including Daoist breath control. Of the adepts (still referred to here as fangshi) at the court of the Wei Kingdom early in the third century C.E., for example, "[Kan] Shih is able to move his ch'i [qi] and perform tao-yin [daoyin] exercises, [Tso] Tz'u is enlightened about the [sexual] arts 'within the chamber,' and [Xi] Chien is good at avoiding [eating] grains. They all claim to be three hundred years old."[34] A text called the *Laixiangji*, which may date from the fourth century, listed no fewer than thirty-six different methods for nourishing one's nature and attaining immortality, ranging from "breathing and visualizing the cinnabar field" to "using sacrifices to bring spirits" and eremitism. Qigong mixed freely with cabalistic ideas and talismanic beliefs: the medieval Daoists "also make seals of wood, engraving stars, planets, the sun and moon upon them; and, inhaling ch'i [qi] and grasping them, they use them to seal a disease, curing many."[36]

Some believe incense lifts prayers to heaven. In the Daoist tradition, individuals can also be found practicing various exercises for health and spiritual development. Some are obviously martial. Symbolically, incense can represent the movement of qi.

In the Han and pre-Han periods qigong had enjoyed a preeminent position among the arts of longevity. When asked for the secret of his long life by Emperor Wen early in the second century B.C.E., for example, the 180-year-old Duke Dou supposedly replied: "Your servant [practices] tao-yin [daoyin]; it is not that I have taken any potions."[37] In the immortality cult that flowered after the fall of the Han, however, it was the elixir of immortality which eclipsed qigong.[38]

Chinese elixirs apparently originated with the shaman's use of intoxicants in antiquity to induce trances. The drugs used for that purpose may have included alcohol, hallucinogenic mushrooms, and other less well-defined "medicines."[39] The *Shanhaijing*, for example, speaks of a mountain where no fewer than ten shamans "rise and descend, gathering the hundred medicines."[40] This use of drugs was then picked up and elaborated on by the fangshi of the early Imperial era, and emerged as the path of choice to immortality in the third century C.E.

The ingredients of medieval immortality potions included fungi and some thing known as the "five mineral" powder.[41] Gold was another favorite substance. With typical literal-mindedness some Daoists reasoned that since "it is in the nature of gold that it does not decay .... [so, too,] when the alchemist consumes it he obtains immortality."[42] However, it was the "refinement of cinnabar" (*liandan*) that was most esteemed by serious adherents of the immortality cult. Cinnabar (HgS, or mercuric sulfide), in fact, came to be a veritable synonym for the elixir itself, and it was in the shadow of that mighty potion that by the sixth century qigong came to be known as *neidan*, or "internal cinnabar," in selfconscious imitation of the more important "external cinnabar" (*waidan*) which was the elixir of immortality itself.[43]

It may strike the reader as odd that intelligent literati were so credulous as to believe in physical immortality. Not all were, but China did have a long tradition of belief in ancestral spirits, ghosts, and other such things. In this the Chinese cannot be said to have been any more credulous than other peoples, but the Chinese were also "rational" enough to question whether it was possible for spirits to exist apart from the material world. Prior to the introduction of the Buddhist belief in reincarnation, therefore, many Chinese suspected that at death "the body and spirit were extinguished together" or at least that their residue was transformed into new material objects.[44] A non-corporeal immortality of the soul in the Christian sense was simply inconceivable, but, this did not mean that spirits did not exist.[45] Like the air itself, which was also composed of physical matter, they were ethereal but physical beings invisible to mortal eyes.[46]

"Immortals" (*xian*), then, were simply deathless spiritual beings who belonged to a more rarefied sphere of matter than mankind.[47] Since all objects in the universe were constructed of a single basic substance, and since all things were in a constant process of transformation, it followed that almost anything could theoretically be transformed into almost anything else if only the necessary preconditions could be met.⁴⁸ As Tung Jungchang (179-219) wrote, "Those who attain the Tao [Dao] sprout pinions on their arms, long feathers on their bellies, fly the unsealable blue sky, and pass over the interminable affairs of this world."⁴⁹ Medicine seemed a reasonable catalyst for this change, moreover, since the relentless Han expectation of natural symmetry implied that if there were drugs that could kill people, as there certainly were, there should also be corresponding drugs that were antidotes for death.⁵⁰

Unfortunately, the medicines that medieval alchemists brewed often proved harmful or fatal to those who consumed them.⁵¹ It was not unnatural, under the circumstances, for skeptics to point to the absence of evidence for success and wonder, if it were really possible to attain immortality, where all the immortals were.⁵²

In his "Essay on Nourishing Life" (*Yang Sheng Lun*), Xi Kang (223-262) began cautiously:

> In this world there are those who say that immortality can be obtained through study, and that through effort one can avoid death. There are others who say that a maximum age of 120 has been the same in antiquity and modern times, and that going beyond this is always a fantastic delusion. Both of these [positions] neglect the facts.⁵³

For Xi the records of immortals in the old histories were proof enough that immortals had actually existed, but he then went on to suggest that they must have been "specially endowed with a different" qi. For modern man to attain immortality, while still theoretically within the realm of possibility, was practically out of reach. Instead, Xi's recipe for nourishing life in the modern world was simply to harmonize with the Dao, consume medicines and drink wine, and nestle into calm inactivity. "Forget enjoyment, and then your pleasure will be sufficient. Neglect life, and then your body will be preserved."⁵⁴ In the classic Daoist paradox, since the Dao works through a process of reversal, "those who do not treat life as valuable are the ones who excel at valuing life."⁵⁵

Although Xi Kang did believe in immortals and was actually one of the more prominent third century enthusiasts for collecting medicines and methods of mental and physical self-cultivation, he also clearly possessed a healthy dose of skepticism and had a realistic sense of the possibilities.[56] In the sixth century, Xi's caution was echoed by Yan Chidui (531-591), who advised his sons to avoid the futile search for immortality but conceded that nourishing the spirit, breath control, and the proper use of medicine could result in longer life.[57]

The most ardent seekers of immortality were apologetic. In the second century, the *Taipingjing* warned that "[some] doctors and shamans only want to get people's money."[58] The royal family of third century Wei, who had summoned an assortment of fangshi to their court, explained that, of course, "we all consider this to be laughable and do not put any credence in it."[59] And in the most famous of all collections of formulas for immortality, the author of the fourth century *Baopuzi* protested with evident embarrassment that he only wanted "to treat the logic in things exhaustively."[60]

With the waning of the medieval social order after the late Tang dynasty (618-907), the immortality cult gradually diminished in importance. Internal self-cultivation through qigong, often referred to during this period as neidan, largely superseded the consumption of elixirs.[61] The mainstream of elite scholar-official interest in the late Imperial period was diverted away from overt religious enthusiasms towards secular Neo-Confucianism, but the religious nimbus surrounding qigong spread now to China's common people through the rise of new forms of popular sectarian Buddho-Daoist religion.

The most famous of these sects was called the White Lotus Society. This sect claimed to have been founded in the era of division after the fall of the Han, but actually seems not to have reached mature form until as late as the sixteenth century.[62] For our purposes the significant thing about White Lotus sectarian religion is that it taught qigong as part of its repertoire of salvationist techniques.[63] It was out of societies like the White Lotus—if not the White Lotus sect itself—that the historical Chinese martial arts first appeared.

No better illustration of the martial arts in practice can be found than the Boxer uprising that erupted at the beginning of the twentieth century. The reason this is such a fascinating example is that the Boxers' so-called "boxing" really consisted of shamanistic dances for inducing spiritual possession and divine invincibility, and not the kind of martial arts combat we would expect.[64] Nor were the Boxers unique in this respect. In many less well-known martial associations as well, such as the early twentieth century Red Spears studied by Elizabeth Perry, ritual magic seems to have been the most prominent feature.[65] The simple explanation for this is that in premodern China "martial arts" were part of a larger matrix of religious belief and practice and inseparable from that religious context.

In the twentieth century, however, "science" and "democracy" became the new watchwords for educated Chinese youth. During the "New Culture" and "May Fourth" movements that began in World War I, the Chinese intelligentsia attempted to remake completely Chinese culture in the Western image. Old religious practices were denounced as "superstition" and rejected as embarrassing reminders of China's backward feudal past.

Qigong was not discarded during this century of modernization, but it was stripped of its burden of religious "superstition." Today qigong is presented as a part of China's lengthy folk medical tradition.[66] It is now considered a "scientific" rather than a religious technique for curing diseases and lengthening life, and, like so much of China's native medical tradition, it is currently attracting worldwide interest. Exciting, if as yet unverified, successes have been reported in treating such fashionable diseases as cancer using qigong.[67]

It is certainly not an error to treat qigong as a medical technology in this fashion. In the fourth century B.C.E. *Inner Classic of the Yellow Emperor*, for example, the daoyin and xingqi forms of qigong were already listed as varieties of medical treatment alongside moxabustion, massage, acupuncture, and the consumption of drugs.[68] A Daoist adept in the third century southern state of Wu "fasted to await the patient's cure whenever he moved his ch'i [*xingqi*] to treat someone's illness."[69] A sixth-century bibliographic treatise in the *Suishu* even mentions a short book in one scroll, "On Methods of Treatment with Qi" (*Lunqi chi liao fang*).[70] In the medieval immortality cult, however, the healing of diseases was but the first step in a continuum that led eventually to immortality. No clear separation was even conceivable between medicine and religion.

It was out of this same religious matrix that the modern martial arts emerged. The fighter and the healer are bound together by their common religious background and by their shared technology of qigong. Many of the popular martial art forms in late Imperial China, such as *taijiquan* (supreme-ultimate boxing), *xingiquan* (body and thought boxing), and *baguachang* (eight trigrams hands), show clear evidence of qigong influence.[71] Taiji in particular is interesting. It is the quintessential Chinese martial art, but its practice is marked by breath control, concentration, and graceful dance-like movements. The casual Western observer might never even guess that it was supposed to be a form of combat. And yet the experts all insist it is the most deadly martial art of all.[72] If so, this may be because concentration of the kind developed in qigong really is a way to better health, coordination, and keener combat ability. As the Han dynasty thinkers had realized long ago, the mind really can be the key to many things.

NOTES

[1] Joseph Needham, *Science and Civilization in China, Vol. 2* (Cambridge: Cambridge University Press, 1962), 145-6. See also *Wang Hsin-wu, T'ai-chi ch'üan-fa ching-i* (The Essential meaning of the Methods of Taijiquan) (Hong Kong: T'aip'ing shu-chü, 1962), 1.

[2] Li Chih-yung, ed., *Chung-kuo ch'i-kung shih* (A History of Chinese Qi Gong) (Honan: Ho-nan k'o-hsüeh chi-shu ch'upanshe, 1988), 2.

[3] *Meng Tzu* (Mencius), annotated by Chao Ch'i (Ssu-pu ts'ung-kan edition; Shanghai: Shanghai shang-wu yin-shu-kuan, 1929), 3.6b. For Zhu Xi, see Li Chih-yung, 26.

[4] Arthur Waley, *The Way and its Power: A Study of the Tao Te Ching and its Place in Chinese Thought* (Guilford: Billing and Sons, Ltd., 1934), 118.

[5] Derk Bodde, "The Chinese Cosmic Magic Known as Watching for the Ethers," *Essays on Chinese Civilization* (Princeton: Princeton University Press, 1981), 351-52.

[6] T'aip'ing ching ho-chiao (The Collated Classic of Great Peace), ed. by Wang Ming (Peking: Chung-hua shu-chü, 1960), 27.

[7] Murakami Yoshimi, *Chogoku no sennin – Hobokushi no shiso* (Chinese Immortals – the Thought of the Paop'utzu) (Kyoto: Heirakuji shoten, 1956), 139.

[8] See Charles Le Blanc, *Huai Nan Tzu: Philosophical Synthesis in Early Han Thought* (Hong Kong: Hong Kong University Press, 1985), 204; Kenneth De Woskin, *A Song for One or Two: Music and the Concept of Art in Early China*, Michigan Papers in Chinese Studies, No. 42 (Ann Arbor: University of Michigan Center for Chinese Studies, 1982), 38.

[9] *Lieh tzu*, annotated by Chang Chan (c. 340-400) (reprint; Taipei: T'aiwan chung-hua shu-chü, 1982), 1.14a.

[10]   *T'aip'ingching*, 25, 311.

[11] For the words of the gentleman, see Wu Lu-ch'iang and Tenney L. Davis, tr., "An Ancient Chinese Treatise on Alchemy Entitled Ts'an T'ung Ch'i," Isis, 18.2 (1932), 245. Fu Xuan's text on "Rectifying the Mind" is included in *Ch'üan Chin wen* (Complete Writings of the Qin Dynasty), in *Ch'üan shang-ku san-tai Ch'in Han san-kuo liu-ch'ao wen*, ed. by Yen K'o-chün (1762-1843) (reprint; Kyoto: Chobun shuppansha,

1981), 1733.

[12] Li Chih-yung, 9. Murakami Yoshimi defines *xingqi* as "to take in much ch'i [qi] and breathe deeply" (2).

[13] *Chuang tzu tsuan-chien* (The Annotated Zhuang Zi), ed. by Ch'ien Mu (Hong Kong: Tung-nan yin-wu ch'u-pan-she, n.d.), 122. *The Inner Classic of the Yellow Emperor* (Huang-ti nei-ching) also contains important early references to qigong, and may be somewhat older. Francis Rueyshuang Lee suggests it may date from the fourth century B.C.E. (*The "Silent Art" of Ancient China: Historical Analysis of the Intellectual and Philosophical Influences in the Earliest Medical Corpus Ling Shu Ching* [Taipei: Linking Publishing Co., 1980], 46).

[14] Lin Hou-sheng and Lo P'ei-yü, *Chi-kung san-pai wen* (Three Hundred Questions Concerning Qi Gong) (Canton: Kuang-tung k'o-chi ch'upanche, 1983), 5.

[15] Wang Ch'ung (27c. 100 C.E.), *Lun Heng* (An Appraisal of Discussions) (reprint; Taipei: T'ai-wan chung-hua shu-chü, 1981), 7.19b.

[16] See Ishida Hidemi, "Body and Mind: The Chinese Perspective," in *Taoist Meditation and Longevity Techniques*, ed. by Livia Kohn (Ann Arbor: Center for Chinese Studies, University of Michigan, 1989), 45.

[17] *Huang-t'ing ching* (The Classic of the Yellow Court), quoted in T'ao Hung-ching (456-536 C.E.), *Yang-hsing yen-ming lu* (A Record of Cultivating Nature and Prolonging Life), in *Tao-tsang yang-sheng shu shih-chung*, ed. by Li Shih-hua and Shen Te-hui (Peking: Chung-i ku-chi ch'upanshe, 1987), 5.

[18] *Ts'e-fu yuan-keui* (The Great Tortoise of the Archives) (c. 1013) (reprint; Taipei: T'ai-wan chung-hua shu-chü, 1981), 836.9917.

[19] The importance of thought in qigong is eloquently stated in Miura Kunio, "The Revival of Qi: Qigong in Contemporary China," in Kohn, ed., *Taoist Meditation*, 337.

[20] Murakami Yoshimi, 147. Daoist concentration is described in Li Chih-yung, 96 ff.

[21] Ko Hung (c. 280-340), *Paop'utzu* (The Master Embracing Simplicity) (reprint; Taipei: T'aiwan chung-hua shu-chü, 1984), nei-p'ien 15. 7a-8a.

[22] Chang Chungyuan ("An Introduction to Taoist Yoga," *The Review of Religion*, 20.3-4 [1956]) tentatively asserts the relative priority of indigenous Chinese techniques.

[23] For An Shihgao, see Tsukamoto Zenryu, "The Early Stages in the Introduction of Buddhism into China (Up to the Fifth Century A.D.)," *Cahiers d'histoire mondials*, 5.3 (1960), 557.

24 The modern martial arts are often closely associated with Buddhism – especially through the Shaolin school in China and Zen in Japan – but this is actually a perversion of the important Buddhist belief in pacifism and can be explained in part as a result of a strong Daoist influence. See Paul Demieville, "Le bouddhisme et la guerre," *Choix d 'etudes bouddhiques* (Leiden: E.J. Brill, 197 3), 288 and passim.

25 *P'eng Tsu ching* (The Classic of Peng Zu), in *Yang-hsing yen-ming lu*, 14. The text is ascribed to the late Han by Catherine Despeux, "Gymnastics: The Ancient Tradition," in Kohn, ed., *Taoist Meditation*, 229.

26 A link between these fangshi and the older practices of shamanism has been observed by Li Fengmao ("Fu-Ch'u-tz'u te k'ao-ch'a chih-i" [Personal Adornment, the Consumption of Medicine, and Shamanistic Tradition: An Investigation of the Ch'u Tz'u from the Perspective of Shamanism], *Ku-tien wenhsueh*, 3 [1981], 89) and others. For shamanism, see Edwin D. Harvey, "Shamanism in China," *Studies in the Science of Society*, ed. by George Peter Murdock (New Haven: Yale University Press, 1937). For the rise of fangshi, see Ku Mingchien (Ku Chiehkang), *Ch'in Han te fangshih yü ju-sheng* (Qin and Han fangshi and Confucians) (1933; Taipei: Li-jen shu-chü, 1985), 11. Ssuma Ch'ien (145-90 B.C.) ascribed the deceits of fangshi to a misunderstanding of the scientific principle of the succession of yin and yang. See *Shih-chi* (Records of the Grand Historian) (Peking: Chung-hua shu-chü, 1959), 1368-69.

27 Michael Strickmann, "On the Alchemy of T'ao Hung-ching," in *Facets of Taoism: Essays in Chinese Religion*, ed. by Holmes Welch and Anna Seidel (New Haven: Yale University Press, 1979), 165.

28 *T'ai-p'ing kuang-chi* (Extensive Records of the Taiping Era), ed. by Li Fang (925-996) (reprint; Peking: Chung-hua chu-chü, 1981), 55-56.

29 Yü-chih-t'ang t'an-hui (Clustered Conversations of the Jade and Iris Hall), ed. by Hsü Yün-lin (fl. c. 1616) (1875 edition), 17.21a.

30 *T'ai-p'ing kuang-chi*, 56.

31 *T'ai-p'ing ching*, 403.

32 *Yu-chün nien-p'u* (A Chronicle of the General of the Right), ed. by Lu I-t'ung, Mei-shu ts'ung-shu 4.9 (1855; Taipei: I-wen yin-shu-kuan, n.d.), 370.

33 Tsukamoto Zenryu, *Shina bukkyoshi kenkyo, hoku-gi hen* (Studies in the History of Chinese Buddhism, the Northern Wei Chapters) (Tokyo: Kobunto shobo, 1942), 49.

34 Ch'en Shou (233-97), *San-kuo shih* (The Annals of the Three Kingdoms) (Peking: Chung-hua shu-chü, 1959), 29.805.

35 This text is quoted in *Ch'u-hsüeh chi* (A Record for Initial Study), edited by Hsü Chien (659-729) (reprint; Peking: Chung-hua shu-chü, 1962), 23.549- 50. The work is otherwise unknown and undatable, but Lai-hsiang was a place name in the Qin dynasty.

36 Wei Cheng (580-643), ed., *Sui-shu* (History of the Sui Dynasty) (reprint; Peking: Chung-hua shu-chü, 1973), 35.1093.

37 Huan T'an (43 B.C.-28 C.E.), *Huan tzu hsin-lun* (New Essays of Master Huan) (reprint; Taipei: T'aiwan chung-hua shu-chü, 1976), 1 lb. Different versions of the story are in circulation.

38 According to Murakami Yoshimi (143), spiritual immortality could be attained by union with the Dao through meditation, but immortality of the body required the consumption of medicines, swallowing qi, and so on.

39 See Chang Kwang-chih, *Art, Myth, and Ritual: The Path to Political Authority in Ancient China* (Cambridge: Harvard University Press, 1983), 55; Michael Strickmann, *Notes on Mushroom Cults in Ancient China* (Ghent: Rijksuniversiteit, 1966).

40 *Shan hai ching chiao-chu* (The Collated and Annotated Classic of Mountains and Seas) (date uncertain), ed. by Yuan K'o (Shanghai: Shanghai kuchi ch'upanshe, 1980), 16.396.

41 Chang Hua (232-300), *Po-wu chih* (An Account of Diverse Phenomena) (reprint; Taipei: T'aiwan chung-hua shu-chü, 1983), 7.lb. The so-called "five mineral powder" is discussed in Kuo Lin-ko, "Wei Chin feng-liu" (The Fashions of the Wei and Chin), *Chung-kuo hsüeh-pao*, 1.6 (1944), 48.

42 *Ts'an t'ung ch'i k'ao-i* (An Examination of Variants in the Covenant of the Union of the Three) (c. 142), ed. by Zhu Xi (reprint; Taipei: T'aiwan chung-hua shu-chü, 1983), 12a.

43 For the appearance of the term *neidan*, see Ko Chao-kuang, *Tao-chiao yü chung-kuo wen-hua* (Daoism and Chinese Culture), Chung-kuo wen-huashih ts'ung-shu (Shanghai: Shang-haijen-min ch'upanshe, 1987), 110. Isabelle Robinet ("Original Contributions of Neidan to Taoism and Chinese Thought," in Kohn, ed., *Taoist Meditation*, 301) limits the designation neidan to only those texts actually using chemical terminology, but clearly the comparison with laboratory alchemy helped shape the identity of qigong practice in general during this period.

44 Cheng Tao-tzu (5th century), "Shen pu mieh lun" (On the Non-Extinction of the Spirit), contained in *Hung ming chi* (The Collection Expanding Illumination), ed. by Seng Yu (435-518) (reprint; Taipei: T'aiwan chung-hua shu-chü, 1983), 5.2a. Cheng, of course, argues for

the Buddhist position. For a classic description of the process of death, see *Lieh tzu*, 1.9b.

45 Donald Holzman (*La vie et la pensee de Hi K'ang* [223-262 Ap. J.-C.] [Leiden: E. J. Brill, 1957], 53) observes that for the third century Chinese "une immortalite sans le corps est impensable [immortality with the body is unthinkable]."

46 The discussant in Hui-yuan's (334-416) "Sha-men pu ching wang che lun" (Sramana Are Not Those Who Honor Kings) (*Hung ming chi*, 5.9a) offers the apparently trite opinion that "although the spirit is a subtle thing, it is certainly still something that is transformed by yin and yang." As much as the coarsest of substances, spirits too were part of the physical world.

47 See Nathan Sivin, *Chinese Alchemy: Preliminary Studies* (Cambridge: Harvard University Press, 1968), 41; Yü Yingshih, "Life and Immortality in the Mind of Han China," *Harvard Journal of Asiatic Studies*, 25 (1965), 88-89.

48 Seev Homer H. Dubs, "The Beginnings of Alchemy, " *Isis*, 38.1-2 (1947), 73, note 76. The third century understanding of fundamental unity amid constant change is noted, for example, in Isabelle Robinet, "Kouo Siang ou le monde comme absolu," *T'oung Pao*, 69.1-3 (1983), 83.

49 *Ch'uan Hou-Han wen* (Complete Writings of the Later Han Dynasty), in *Ch'uan shang-ku san-tai Ch'in Han san-kuo liu-ch'ao wen*, 89.955.

50 The skeptic Huan Tan was told that since "Heaven produced medicines that kill men, there must be medicines to make men live" (*Huan tzu hsin-lun*, 26a) Huan's astute reply was that poisons are not actually medicines to kill people, but rather substances which are simply not appropriate to eat.

51 The effects of taking these drugs have been thoroughly studied in Ho Ping-yü and Joseph Needham, "Elixir Poisoning in Medieval China," *Janus*, 48 (1959).

52 See Xiang Xiu's third century criticism of Xi Kang, translated in Robert G. Henricks, *Philosophy and Argumentation in Third-Century China: The Essays of Hsi K'ang* (Princeton: Princeton University Press, 1983), 35.

53 *Ch'uan san-kuo wen* (Complete Writings of the Three Kingdoms), in *Ch'uan shang-ku san-tai Ch'in Han san-kuo liu-ch'ao wen*, 48.1324.

54 Ibid., 48.1324-25.

55 *Chin-shu* (History of the Qin Dynasty), ed. by Fang Hsüan-ling (578-648) (reprint; Peking: Chung-hua shu-chü, 1974), 49.1370.

56 Xi's thought is discussed in Horiike Nobuo, "Kei Ko ni okeru shinko to shakai: Sho Shu to no 'yojoron' ronso o chushin to shite" (Faith and

Society in Xi Kang-Centering on the Debate with Xiang Xiu over his "Essay on Nourishing Life") *Rekishi ni okeru minshu to bunka: Sakai Tadao sensei koki shukuga kinen ronshu* (Tokyo: Kokusho kankokai, 1982), 109; Holzman, 52-60; and Li Fengmao, "Hsi K'ang yang-sheng ssu-hsiang chih yen-chiu" (Studies of Xi Kang's Thought on Nourishing Life), *Ching-i wen-li hsueh-yuan hsueh-pao*, 2 (1979).

[57] Yen Chih-t'ui [Yan Chi-dui], *Family Instructions for the Yen Clan: Yen shih chia-hsun*, trans., by Teng Ssu-yü (Leiden: E.J. Brill, 1968), 131-133.

[58] *T'ai-p'ing ching*, 620.

[59] *San-kuo chih*, 29.805.

[60] Ko Hung, *Alchemy, Medicine and Religion in the China of A.D. 320: The Nei P'ien of Ko Hung*, trans. by James R. Ware (Dover, 1966), 206.

[61] See Nathan Sivin, "Science and Medicine in Imperial China – The State of the Field," *Journal of Asian Studies*, 47.1 (1988), 55. This movement parallels the simultaneous philosophical shift from Daoist concepts of external transcendence back towards Buddhist and Confucian themes of the immanence of truth within oneself. See Mori Mikisaburo, "Chogoku shiso ni okers choetsu to naizai" (Transcendence and Immanence in Chinese Thought), *Toyo gakujutsu kenkyu*, 23.2 (1984), 124.

[62] For an overview of White Lotus sectarianism, see Susan Naquin, "The Transmission of White Lotus Sectarianism in Late Imperial China," in *Popular Culture in Later Imperial China*, ed. by David Johnson, et al. (Berkeley: University of California Press, 1985).

[63] The use of qigong in the White Lotus movement is described in Daniel L. Overmeyer, *Folk Buddhist Religion: Dissenting Sects in Late Traditional China* (Cambridge: Harvard University Press, 1976), 188, 190-92; Naquin, 275.

[64] See Kobayashi Kazumi, "Giwandan no minsho shiso" (The Popular Thought of the Boxers), in *Koza Chogoku kingendai-shi 2: giwandan undo* (Tokyo: Tokyo daigaku shuppankai, 1978), 243.

[65] Elizabeth J. Perry, *Rebels and Revolutionaries in North China, 1845-1945* (Stanford: Stanford University Press, 1980), 186-197.

[66] See Linda Chih-ling Koo, Nourishment of Life: The Culture of Health in Traditional Chinese Society (Ph.D. dissertation, University of California; Ann Arbor: University Microfilms, 1976), 71-72. Lin Hou-sheng (1), for example, introduces qigong as one of China's folk medical practices.

[67] Cui Lili ("Fitness and Health through Qigong," *Beijing Review* 32.17 [April 24-30, 1989]: 20, 22) reports that qigong has successfully been used to treat "terminal cancer patients" in the People's Republic. It is

not clear yet how credible such claims are.

[68] *Ling-shu ching* (The Classic of the Spiritual Axis), in *Huang-ti su-wen ling-shu ching* (The Yellow Emperor's Classics of Common Questions and the Spiritual Axis), annotated by Wang Ping (Ssu-pu ts'ung-k'an edition; Shanghai: Shang-hai shang-wu yin-shu-kuan, 1929), 7.3a.

[69] *Pao-p'u tzu, nei-p'ien* 15.3a.

[70] *Sui-shu*, 34.1046.

[71] See Li Chih-yung, 3 92. Nathan Sivin ("Science and Medicine," 68) notes real differences between taijiquan and the ancient daoyin exercises, however.

[72] For the effectiveness of taijiquan in martial arts competition, see "Fang t'ai-chi ta-shih Wang P'ei-sheng), *Jen-min jih-pao* (People's Daily), overseas edition, Aug. 3, 1987, 2.

chapter 3

Sohei: The Warrior Monks of Old Japan

by Jerry Shine

The restoration of Japan's samurai so dominates the country's feudal past that it's easy to forget that at one time there was another force in Japan that rivaled even them: the sohei, or warrior monks. Photos courtesy of the Imperial Household Agency.

From the tenth through the thirteenth century, the sohei were an awesome spectacle for the Japanese people to behold. When they felt they had been wronged, they marched down from their temples by the thousands, their lines stretching out along the roads leading into the capital city of Kyoto as far as the eye could see. As they marched, they chanted in unison for the punishment of their enemies, whom they chose strictly on the basis of their immediate political or financial needs. Religious matters were of little import to the sohei and to prove the justness of their cause, they were willing to make any argument, no matter how outrageous. At one point, the demands of the sohei from a temple in Yamashima became so exasperating that the Emperor Shirakawa (1053-1129) began to use the term "Yamashima logic" to describe all cases of ridiculous reasoning. While their reasoning may have been absurd, their physical appearance and abilities were anything but. Wearing hooded Buddhist robes over their battle armor, brandishing naginata, a vicious weapon particularly effective in open areas, and carrying *mikoshi*—the portable shinto shrines still seen today—one can only imagine the terror they inspired in the Japanese people, commoners and aristocrats alike. These guardians of the country's spiritual safety appeared suddenly, by the thousands, vowing to bring down not only the wrath of the gods to whom they prayed but also the more immediate threat of their own physical violence. To the often effeminate aristocrats of Kyoto, who normally only heard reports of peasant uprisings in far-off parts of the country, this was no doubt a frightening confrontation with the violent side of life.

Looking at the serenity of Japan's Buddhist monks today it's difficult to imagine the sohei as their forefathers. Brutal and warlike, petty and quick to anger, having strayed far from their Buddhist tenets of peace but believing in their own righteousness every bit as much as the Christian priests who once carried out the Inquisition, the sohei were spawned from the same social conditions that created the samurai.

At the time of Buddhism's introduction to Japan, the road to priesthood was a difficult one. Before a man could apply for the government examination to become a monk, a minimum of three years of study under a qualified priest was required; entire texts had to be memorized, a full understanding of Buddhist concepts acquired. If he passed the test, another three years of study were required before he could be ordained, at which time he was given over two hundred admonitions, including prohibitions against killing and the possession of weapons.

By the ninth century, however, a severe shortage of monks to administer to the country's spiritual needs, combined with an intense desire among peasants to enter the priesthood and escape the drudgery of everyday life, resulted in such a deterioration of standards that few of those ordained were qualified either spiritually or intellectually. By the tenth and eleventh centuries, it wasn't only peasants who flocked to the priesthood, but the samurai of low-ranking families who had little hope of advancing in the country's stultified social system.

Sohei of the Enrykuji Temple plan
an attack on the Onjoji temple.
Print published between 1192-1333.

The rapidly changing nature of Japan's society was just as important to the development of the sohei. In the tenth century, after three hundred years of living in the shadow of China, studying her culture and emulating her ways, Japan cut off all contact with her. The Japanese began to strike out on their own, and in the cultural centers of the country, aristocrats created new forms of literature, painting, sculpture and architecture, all of which were distinctly Japanese, many of which would be admired for centuries to come.

Outside of the capital, however, throughout the rest of the country, powerful clans were laying the structure for a warlike society that would last almost as long. All of the land in Japan theoretically belonged to the Imperial Family, but it was run by the various clans, who controlled the peasants and then paid taxes on it. As the Court grew more and more decadent, the clans grew more powerful and they were soon able to donate large tracts of farm land to select monasteries and declare them tax-exempt. In a country where four-fifths of the land is mountainous, and only one-fifth suitable for farming, this was no petty act.

Eventually, the clans and monasteries became so powerful that they were virtually autonomous governments and were forced to build up private armies to protect their estates—first from the government, then from each other. In the clans, these soldiers evolved into the samurai. In the monasteries, they became the sohei.

All of these factors—the sohei's lack of spirituality, their great numbers, the exalted position they held in society, and the need to defend their property—led them away from the world of spiritual freedom and into one of corruption, deceit and arrogance. They evolved from peaceful Buddhist monks, and almost from the start they set out on a path for their own destruction at the hands of the samurai.

The three major sohei temples of the period were the Enryakuji Temple, the Kofukuji Temple, and the Todaji Temple. Each maintained several thousand warrior monks along with large retinues of servants and peasants.

In the tenth century, the sohei had already aligned themselves in an adversarial stance based on threats and intimidation against the power structure of society, even as the samurai were laying the foundation to make themselves not just an essential element of that power structure, but the very structure itself. At the time, Japan was under the control of the Fujiwara clan, which had gained power over the Imperial Family through a system of intermarriage: marrying their daughters to young emperors, encouraging those emperors to retire, and then taking control of their throne and their offspring.

For a Fujiwara, the ultimate punishment was expulsion from the clan, which meant confinement to one's home and banishment from all court appearances. Surprisingly, the power to expel didn't rest with the clan itself, but with a council of priests from several sohei temples. Others were frightened into compliance.

By the end of the eleventh century, the sohei learned to make better use of their religious power and in 1095, angered that a Fujiwara official hadn't been sufficiently punished for an insult, three thousand Enryakuji sohei marched on the capital, carrying, for the first time in history, mikoshi to frighten the Court.

Samurai who supported the Fujiwara met them at the palace. Knowing the fervor of the two groups, we can imagine the scene that must have taken place that day: thousands of armed warriors; swords, naginata, and mikoshi gleaming in the sun; deafening chants. Faced with the frightening spectacle of the mikoshi, which were believed to contain the country's shinto deities, the samurai tried to hold the sohei back without using force, but when it became clear that they couldn't, skirmishes broke out, a mikoshi was destroyed, and the result was a fullfledged riot. Individually, the sohei were brutal fighters but as a combined force they lacked the military discipline and training of the samurai and were no match for their tactical strength. The samurai drove them from the palace.

A week later, the samurai who had been in charge at the palace gate that day were imprisoned, the Fujiwara official about whom the sohei had originally complained was sent into exile, and the abbot of the Enryakuji Temple was stripped of his position and taken into custody. But while he was being escorted back to the capital by a group of samurai, the sohei attacked again and brought him back to Enryakuji. Despite furious Imperial orders to return him, they refused, and rather than allow more fighting to break out, the government let the matter be forgotten.

The sohei of the Kofukuji Temple carried into battle not mikoshi, but *shinboku*, the branches of sacred trees in which deities were also believed to live. Since damage to a shinboku would incur untold natural disasters, the demands of the Kofukuji sohei were also usually met, albeit reluctantly.

Sohei, at far right, and court nobles attend the Emperor Shirakawa.

There were battles in which the sohei defeated the samurai, but only when they outnumbered them. More often, the samurai drove them from the capital. But the sohei believed fervently in their own righteousness and the defeat would not stop them from marching into the capital again at the next convenient time.

The Court wasn't the only target of their attacks. The sohei of various temples often fought amongst themselves over land and personnel disputes—rarely, if ever, over religious issues. These battles broke out for the slightest of reasons, such as the servants of one temple being insulted by the servants of another, and without the calming influence of the Court, these battles were even more brutal than those with the samurai. When the sohei fought each other, the goal was total destruction. Fire was their main weapon. In one instance, the Enryakuji sohei attacked the smaller Onjoji Temple and burned more than three hundred buildings to the ground, and more than 24,000 books to ashes. When the battles became so destructive that even the lives of non-religious people were affected, government troops would step in to stop them.

Eventually, toward the end of the twelfth century, the sohei became so embroiled in the military and political affairs of the country that the son of a retired emperor plotted with them to decimate the Taira clan, the most powerful in Japan at the time. Two of the three temples that were asked to give their support agreed. In the end, the uprising was defeated and the influence of the sohei kept in check. At the same time, the Zen School of Buddhism was spreading throughout Japan, emphasizing a harmony with nature and a strict mental discipline; themes which were not only contrary to the sohei mentality, but which eventually provided a foundation for the samurai's stoic philosophy of life.

The sohei continued as a military force, but by the end of the thirteenth century their power had begun to wane even as that of the samurai continued to grow. While the sohei immersed themselves in petty political squabbles, the samurai were embracing self-discipline, indifference to suffering, and physical and mental toughness as the marks of their strength. They were beginning to look on the sword as the soul of their warrior class. The sohei weren't supported agriculturally by the peasants to the same extent as the samurai and were not able to devote their lives to the perfection of martial skills. But more importantly, they never developed a philosophical code, such as *bushido*, to guide them through the country's warring periods.

The sohei's last grasp at greatness occurred late in the fourteenth century when several of their temples joined forces with a group of samurai clans and a retired emperor, known posthumously as Daigo II, to revolt against the Hojo Shogunate. The revolt was successful, but one of the samurai leaders, Ashikaga Takauji, seized power for himself and drove Daigo II out of Kyoto.

Toward the end of the sixteenth century, most of the remaining sohei temples were burned to the ground when they tried to interfere with military leaders who were more concerned with strategic geographic positions than they were with religious superstitions. By the end of the century, Toyotomi Hideyoshi, one of Japan's greatest generals, had united the country under one government. In 1588, he passed the Sword Hunt Edict, which made it illegal for anyone other than samurai to possess weapons. The largest sohei temples had already been destroyed. Now, deprived of their naginata and overwhelmed by the increasing number of monks who rejected their values, the sohei soon dwindled away and became just another relic of Japan's feudal past.

REFERENCES

SANSOM, G. (1961). *A history of Japan to 1334*. Stanford, California: Stanford University Press.

TURNBULL, S. R. (1982). *The book of the samurai: The warrior class of Japan*. London: Bison Books.

REISCHAUER, E. (1964). *Japan, Past and present*. New York: Alfred A. Knopf.

chapter 4

Silat Kebatinan as an Expression of Mysticism and Martial Culture in Southeast Asia

by Mark V. Wiley

Illustrations by Carlos Aldrete.

Since it is embraced in wrappings spun by various religious sects, the full significance of *kebatinan* may be obscured even though it maintains its sociocultural identity. Although kebatinan is the final stage of one's study of the indigenous martial art known as *silat* (Draeger and Smith, 1980; Maliszewski, 1992; Sheikh, 1994), its practice is not limited to the *pesilat* (ind., practitioner of silat).[1] Adding to this confusion is the fact that one's kebatinan practice may be steeped in Islam, Hinduism, Buddhism, or any other religious or mystical movement—or variation thereof—including the practice of black and white magic, although such magical practices are frowned upon by the "true" possessor of kebatinan (Stange, 1980; Sheikh, 1994). In fact, as Mulder (1982: 105) notes: "Basically, kebatinan is mysticism, the penetration and the knowledge of the universe with the purpose of establishing a direct relationship between the individual and the sphere of That-Which-Is-Almighty."

It is at this time that I make the distinction between kebatinan movements and variants. A kebatinan movement can be any "school" of thought rooted in a specific religion such as Hinduism, for example. Conversely, variants include those "schools" whose disciples actively depart from the traditional norms of their religion for personal gain, a practice that may constitute a violation of their major religious code.[2] This characterization of kebatinan may not necessarily be accepted by all those who practice it. However, since I neither practice kebatinan nor have witnessed its effects in person,[3] this is how I can best understand and therefore communicate its essence. As with the explanations of traditional peoples who may describe their mystical expression, this explanation is based on my own ethnocentric, compartmentalized world-view. Therefore, any researcher who may use this thesis as a guide is advised to cross reference my interpretations of the references included herein. Because of the vast number of kebatinan movements observed in Southeast Asia, this treatment will offer a mere overview of three of the more common *aliran* (ind., mystical movements or sects), namely the *abangan*, *santri*, and *sumarah*, while focusing on the aspects of those variants which are relevant to the study of Indo-Malayan martial culture. A more specific example of how mysticism permeates the cultural aspects of Southeast Asian belief systems and everyday life is discussed below.

" . . . kebatinan is . . . a direct relationship between the
individual and the sphere of That-Which-Is-Almighty."
- Mulder (1982: 105)

Aliran Kebatinan: An Overview

Kebatinan (arb., integrated into ind., jav.: *batin*, inner, internal, in the heart, hidden and mysterious; *kebatinan*, the science of the *"batin"*) is observed and practiced in Southeast Asia. It is a spiritual path which seeks to develop an inner tranquility through one's total submission and self-surrender to God—any god. Kebatinan is commonly ascribed to mysticism in general and/or those movements relating to it (Stange, 1980; Mulder, 1982). Although there are many kebatinan movements and variants observed today, the general practice of this Southeast Asian mystical expression can be divided into two basic categories. One type involves the practice of the indigenous Southeast Asian martial art known as *silat*, which involves two dimensions: human (e.g., corporeal) and supernatural (e.g., the spirits of angels or culture heroes). In silat, the acquisition of a mystical "energy" is sought. This "energy" is obtained through the practice of specific breathing exercises known as *dzikir* (Sharif, 1990;[4] Maliszewski, 1992). The other type of mystical expression is solely concerned with the dimensions of God, all upon which an "inner" knowing and/or an "internal" awareness is developed through the strict observance of prayer and ritual. Again, these prayers and rituals may assume any number of forms depending on the faith to which one subscribes and the particular *aliran* of which one is a member.

The *abangan kebatinan* variant is rooted in the animistic aspects of Javanism,[5] in particular the peasant element (Geertz, 1960). Although nominally Muslim, the individuals who follow this variant often find their religious inspiration in the Javanism complex associated with animistic, Hindu, Buddhist magical, mystical, religious elements (Mulder, 1970b). The *abangan* variant, regardless of religious doctrine, connects the sociocultural beliefs with the all-encompassing cosmic order that is "Life." Inspired by the *wayang kulit*[6] depicted in the *Mahabharata*, the *abangan* variant views life in the here and now as a mere shadow of the events occurring on a higher plane (Mangkunagara VII of Surakarta, 1957; Mulder, 1982).

The *santri kebatinan* variant, which is followed by the Islam *putihan*, or strict adherents of Islam, also includes within its practice various elements of Javanism (Mulder, 1970b). This further shows how the practice of this mystical endeavor can at times be directed toward a closer relationship with God through a specific religious realm (e.g., Islam) and at other times step outside of the pertinent religious ideals to achieve the goals of the individual practitioner. According to Geertz

(1960: 6), the *santri* variant of kebatinan represents "a stress on the Islamic aspects of the syncretism and is generally related to the trading element [merchant class] (and to certain elements in the peasantry as well)."

The variant known as *sumarah kebatinan*, not unlike other variants, is said to cultivate a state of total surrender or submission, the inwardly receptive state of being (Stange, 1980). However, whereas other variants seem to deal predominantly with a state of internal awareness and self-control, the sumarah movement attempts to direct its energies at changing social patterns in an effort to invoke a greater communal harmony. Indonesians view sumarah kebatinan as a mechanism which enables them to focus on the social interactions which exist between group consciousness and one's culture at large (Stange, 1981).

Kebatinan as Worldview

Worldview can be thought of as the way in which a people view the world, the customs and beliefs of other people, and their relation to the supernatural. Worldview is an all-encompassing, abstract framework for one's life experiences and for ones interpretations of those experiences. Indeed, worldview and religion in Southeast Asia are at once inseparable and syncretic, as noted by Mulder (1970a: 79):

> In most traditional, rather undifferentiated societies, religious practice and belief still provide most of the vital coordinates of a worldview. The sociological and psychological importance of a worldview is that it shapes the attitude of life of individuals; a worldview can therefore be studied as revealing the approach to reality of individuals and groups, which means that it can be analyzed as the logic behind a social system and its dynamics.

However, one distinction needs to be made concerning the observance of religion proper and kebatinan. Whereas the practice of kebatinan attempts to connect the concept of an "inner" man with God, religion adheres to the necessity of an intermediary between man and God (e.g., a prophet, priest, or the written word as presented in the Holy Bible) (Mulder, 1970b).

Anyone may participate in the practice of kebatinan. It is pursued generally to get away from the oppressive social ties, to attain inner tranquility, and to escape the dogma of organized religions (Mulder, 1970b).

Southeast Asian Martial Culture: An Overview

Perhaps one of the best examples of how kebatinan is expressed is through an analysis of Southeast Asian martial arts forms. Most of our understanding in the West concerning these fighting forms relies strictly upon physical movement. Yet in Asia, physical, philosophical, religious, and spiritual expressions also permeate the practice of martial arts. This is probably best seen in Indonesian and Malayan systems of silat. However, a brief introduction to a discussion of silat in Southeast Asian martial arts is in order.

In general, many Asian martial traditions are believed to have originated in India. This belief is supported by the many martial episodes within the pages of such Indian epics as the *Mahabharata* and *Ramayana*. Since Indonesia has been subjected to the cultural and martial influences of India, China, and Indochina (Draeger, 1972; Draeger and Smith, 1980; Maliszewski, 1992), it is no wonder that its martial culture is laced with a plethora of mystical beliefs and practices. Maliszewski (1987, 1992) further notes that Java, Indonesia's cultural and political core, has always been a center of magical and mystical beliefs. With the gaining of independence from the Dutch in 1949 and the ongoing migrations of the Indo-Malayan peoples, there has developed a very sophisticated Southeast Asian combative form collectively known as *silat*—although there are literally hundreds of silat variants or styles practiced on the Indonesian Archipelago and the Malay Peninsula. Because West Java is the current hub of Indonesian silat, it is no surprise that this martial tradition maintains the practice of kebatinan as its highest level.

Although other combatives are found in this geographic region, e.g., *pukulan*, *kuntao*, and various "endemic" forms, Draeger (1972), Stange (1980), and Maliszewski (1987, 1992) note that silat is, in fact, the major self-defense system practiced and the one with the strongest spiritual, religious, and mystical roots. "As a formal tradition, spiritual components of silat are known to have developed through contact with Hindu and Islamic teachings" (Maliszewski, 1992: 27). Draeger (1972) expounds on this idea by asserting that in ancient times the *pendeta* (ind., priests) used to study animal movements from which contemporary silat derives much of its physical form. He further notes that it was the combination of the physical animal actions coupled with various meditative postures which provided the priests with the necessary skills of self-defense. These meditative postures and other spiritual practices were said to have derived from the Tantric and Sufi traditions (Stange, 1980).

The initiation into and the practice of silat are an interesting progression of patience, ritual, and physicality. Draeger and Smith (1980) note that a prospective student must first negotiate with a silat *guru* (ind., teacher) in order to be accepted as his pupil. The pupil must then adhere to tradition by carrying five offerings to the guru at his training pavilion. These offerings include, but are not limited to, a chicken whose blood is spread on the training ground as a symbolic substitute for blood that might otherwise come from the student and a roll of white cloth in which to wrap the corpse if a student should die in training. After a student has been accepted into a particular silat system, he would then undergo a strenuous training progression, which would include the practice of various stances, postures, strikes, blocks, memorized patterns of movements, and sparring practice (Draeger, 1972; Draeger and Smith, 1980; Stange, 1980; Maliszewski, 1987, 1992). The idea is that the student of silat is naive and young (in a spiritual sense) and must, therefore, develop him/herself from the outside in (i.e., from the physical plane to the spiritual dimension).

Silat Kebatinan

Not unlike the corporeal practice of silat, the acquisition of silat kebatinan (e.g., mystical/spiritual training after mastery of the physical art) is gained through a series of progressive stages. As noted by Maliszewski (1992: 28), "[M]ethods of spiritual development resemble the path of silat in many ways, such as . . . moving from external concerns in the world to inner development, importance given to the role of guru, and the significance attributed to moral and ethical conduct." With silat kebatinan, the focus is placed not on physical skills but on inner development which at once transcends the material world and controls it. Again, this mystical path is not necessarily concurrent with all kebatinan movements. Rather, it is determined by the individual aliran or variant thereof to which one subscribes.

The path of silat kebatinan stresses the *rasa* (ind., jav., intuitive inner feeling) and *sujud* (ind., jav., self-surrender). To effect these qualities the practitioner rids himself of earthly habits and desires by emptying his ego so as to be open to receive the divine presence of God, the revelation of the divine residing within the heart (*batin*) (Maliszewski, 1992). The most important attribute of the pesilat is the ethical understanding of his every action. The pesilat fears the outcome of being put in a position of ever having to employ his deadly martial skills. As a result of possessing and developing these God-given fighting abilities, the pesilat, through the prayers associated with silat kebatinan, always holds sacred the qualities of being gracious and merciful.

In silat kebatinan, the *pikiran* (ind., mind) and the *batin* (heart) are never separated. In silat kebatinan, the body (external) is believed to be controlled by the mind, while the feelings (internal) are controlled by the heart. It is generally believed that, if negativity is cultivated from the onset, then the pesilat will be in constant conflict with himself. The biggest war is that which is fought within. If the pesilat can control the internal war, then the external poses no real threat to him. From another perspective, the inner man is conceived of as a microcosm (jav., *jagat cilik*) of the macrocosm (jav., *jagat gede*) that is life (Mulder, 1970b). The practitioner of kebatinan seeks to cultivate the true self (jav., *ingsun gede*), achieving harmony and ultimately unity with this all-encompassing principle (jav., *manunggaling kawulagusti*) as well as with his origin and his destination (jav., *sangkan-paran*). In this final process, the adept becomes one with ultimate reality (Mulder, 1970a). While the attainment of proficiency in corporeal silat may seem rather rudimentary, the path of silat kebatinan is quite strenuous. Overcoming one's attachment to the outward aspects of existence (ind., jav., *lahir*) is no easy attainment and may involve ascetic practices (jav., *tapa*) such as fasting, prayer, mediation (particularly visual concentrative techniques), sexual abstinence, remaining awake throughout the night, or retreating to the mountains and into caves (Maliszewski, 1992). Since this type of practice requires a mode of perseverance and discipline that is demanding, it can be understood why kebatinan is left to the final stage of silat training—the training environment of a *pendekar*[7] (ind., malay, fighter; old jav., skilled duelist, spiritualist).

Haung Tuah is credited as the bearer of the first kris which was said to have no sheath or scabbard. He considered an enemy's body its only sheath.

A common attribute associated with Southeast Asian martial culture is the combination of physical training and occult skills (Draeger, 1972; Draeger and Smith, 1980). These skills include qualities such as invulnerability (jav., *kekebalan*), the ability to fight reflexively, without thought (jav., *kadigdayan*), the ability to withstand a dagger's thrust into the abdomen, and the ability to push or kill at a distance (Draeger, 1972; Draeger and Smith, 1980; Maliszewski, 1987, 1992; Sheikh, 1994). Often, these skills are closely related with the possession of power objects (ind., *jimat*). These amulets may take the form of gemstones, carriages, birds, or kris (jav., dual-edged, serpentine dagger). Whatever the object, its power (jav., *kasekten*) has been attributed to the infusion of living spirit (Stange, 1980). There is one kris in particular, known as the *taming sari* (ind., shielded fruit), which is currently in the possession of the Malayan royal courts. This kris was purportedly made by a man's bare hands, without the aid of water to reduce its temperature, for the legendary Huang Tuah[8] during the fourteenth century. This dagger is said to possess its rightful heir with the spirit power of this culture hero, thus making the holder invincible in battle[9] (Draeger and Smith, 1980; Sheikh, 1994).

Perhaps the most demanding aspect of martial training is the necessity of one's strict adherence to prayer. Primary to the prayer is one's unconditional commitment to God. This commitment is made by way of a vow through the guidance of one's guru. Pesilat and pendekar alike view the consequence of not fully committing to the vow as a serious breach with God.[10] These vows might include the reciting of 70,000 phrases from the Koran, twelve per day. This recitation can not be taken lightly for if one is up to 60,000 recitations and forgets to continue the next day he must begin all over again with phrase one.[11]

To this end, in some systems of silat, breathing is related to meditative aspects which stem from the heart (*batin*) whereas other systems stress the region of the abdomen just below the navel (Draeger, 1972; Draeger and Chambers, 1972). The emphasis placed upon "energy" or "inner power" (ind., *ilmu kebatinan*; jav., *ngelmu kebatinan*) will also vary from one system to another (Maliszewski, 1992). The purification achieved through *tapa* may lead to *semadi* (skt., *samadhi*; jav., ind., *samadi*), a state of mind best described as "world-detached concentration where one is open to receive divine guidance and knowledge and ultimately the revelation of the mystery of life, origin and destiny" (Maliszewski, 1992: 29). Semadi meditation may be practiced as part of one's silat kebatinan for the express purpose of (1) developing a destructive aim by means of magic, (2) attain a specific positive goal for which greatly enhanced power is needed, (3) experience revelation of the mystery of existence, and (4) achieve ultimate deliverance from all earthly desires (Mangkunagara VII of Surakarta, 1957).

Indeed, the final stage in silat training is kebatinan—a metaphysical, supernatural, phenomenological state of being. Without the acquisition of kebatinan, one's silat is said to be incomplete. Moreover, it seems that the pendekar becomes a spiritualist first and a pesilat second. This is understood to mean that the true possession of kebatinan places one beyond the material realms and cultural constraints of this world. Unlike in the West where the Cartesian split exists between mind, body, and spirit, religious practices permeate all aspects of culture and existence in the East. Even in the more base forms of physical expression (e.g., fighting skills) the role accorded to kebatinan was paramount. In the West, the impact of silat has only stressed the physical skill component of a rich tradition. The purpose of this paper has been to document the importance of kebatinan in general and to acquaint the reader with a brief overview illustrating the pervasiveness of these religious-mystical beliefs in the Southeast Asian martial culture at large.

NOTES

[1] For a good overview of a number of kebatinan variants found in Java, see Clifford Geertz, *The Religion of Java* (1960). For a detailed discussion on the variants found within aliran kebatinan, see Neils Mulder's *Aliran Kebatinan* as an expression of the Javanese worldview (1970b).

[2] Sheikh Shamsuddin (personal communication, March 12, 1994) is a Malaysian-born instructor of Malay *Silat Seni Gayong*. The name of this art form, when translated, describes the progression of this indigenous fighting form. *Silat* refers to the corporeal combative form; *seni* is the fine-tuning or artistic expression of silat; *gayong* is the spiritual dimension, which encompasses the practice of various kebatinan.

[3] Video footage of various silat kebatinan were provided for me by *maha guru* (ind., jav., master teacher) Herman Suwanda of the *silat mande muda* style of Bandung, Indonesia, and by Dr. Michael Maliszewski. These tapes include demonstrations of silat masters chewing and swallowing glass, chewing sharp razor blades, cutting tree leaves and wood with various daggers and swords and hacking their own bodies, as well as rubbing flaming torches on their bare skin, all producing no apparent adverse effects.

⁴ Sulaiman Sharif (personal communications, 1989-1991) stresses that the practice of dzikir breathing is an essential element of the *gayong* (spiritual) stage of Malaysian silat practice. Sulaiman Sharif is a Malaysian born master of Silat Seni Gayong and head of the Silat Seni Gayong America Association.

⁵ Neils Mulder (1970b) describes Javanism as follows: "The Javanese Weltanshauung [Worldview] . . . is based on the conviction of the essential unity of all existence. This worldview is more encompassing than religion: it views human existence with a cosmological context, making life itself a religious experience. In this view of life it is not possible to separate the religious from the nonreligious elements; human existence is inescapably related to supernature and it is senseless to sharply distinguish between here and now and the beyond and timeless" (105).

⁶ For a detailed study of the social, cultural, spiritual components and symbolism of the *wayang kulit* see Mangkunagoro VII of Surakarta's data paper, *On the Wayang Kulit (purwa) and Its Symbolic and Mystical Elements* (1957).

⁷ In silat kebatinan, the title of pendekar connotes one who is a spiritualist and leader or champion who has obtained an understanding of true (inner) knowledge, believed to be derived from a Menangkabau expression, *pandai akal*, literally, "ability and mind"; or *andeka*, derived from *adhika*, skt., "more, surpassing in quality," integrated into malay, here referring to a kind of supernatural power possessed by a *dato* (ind., chief) (Chambers and Draeger, 1978; Draeger, 1972, Maliszewski, 1987, 1992).

⁸ Huang Tuah is credited as the bearer of the first kris which was said to have no sheath or scabbard. Tuah considered an enemy's body its only sheath (Draeger and Smith, 1980; Sheikh, 1994).

⁹ For this perspective in relation to the kris, see Draeger (1972), O'Connor (1975), Garrett and Solymon (1978), and Hamzuri (1984).

¹⁰ Sulaiman Sharif, personal communications, 1989-1991.

¹¹ Sheikh Shamsuddin, personal communication, March 15, 1994.

LANGUAGES

Arabic   arb.
Indonesian   ind.
Sanskrit   skt.
Javanese   jav.

REFERENCES

CHAMBERS, Q., AND DRAEGER, D. (1978). *Javanese silat: The fighting art of perisai diri*. Tokyo: Kodansha.

DRAEGER, D. (1972). *Weapons and fighting arts of the Indonesian archipelago*. Tokyo: Charles E. Tuttle.

DRAEGER, D., AND SMITH, R. (1980). *Comprehensive Asian fighting arts*. Tokyo: Kodansha.

BRONRONWEN, G., AND BRONRONWEN, B. (1978). *The world of the Javanese kris*. Honolulu: Asian Arts press.

GEERTZ, C. (1960). *The religion of Java*. London: Collier-Macmillan Ltd.

HAMZURI, D. (1984). *Keris*. Jakarta: Penerbit Djambatan.

KEYES, C., AND DANIELS, E. (1983). *Karma: An anthropological inquiry*. Berkeley: University of California Press.

MALISZEWSKI, M. (1987). Martial arts: An overview. In Mircea Eliade (Ed.), *The encyclopedia of religion* (Vol. 9, pp. 224-228). New York: Macmillan.

MALISZEWSKI, M. (1992). Medical, healing and spiritual components of Asian martial arts: a preliminary field study exploration. *Journal of Asian Martial Arts, 1* (2), 24-57.

MANGKUNAGARA VII of Surakarta, K.G.P.A.A. (1957). On the wayang kulit (purwa) and its symbolic and mystical elements (Claire Holt, Trans.) (Data Paper, No. 27). Ithaca, New York: Cornell University, Southeast Asia Program, Department of Far Eastern Studies.

MULDER, N. (1970a). A comparative note on the Thai and the Javanese worldview as expressed by religious practice and belief. *Journal of the Siam Society, 58* (2), 79-85.

MULDER, N. (1970b). Aliran kebatinan as an expression of the Javanese worldview. *Journal of Southeast Asian Studies, 1*(2), 105-114.

MULDER, N. (1982). Abangan Javanese religious thought and practice. Bijdragen tot de Taal-, Land- en Volkenkunde, 139, 260-267.

O'CONNOR, S. (1975). Iron working as spiritual inquiry in the Indonesian archipelago. *History of Religions, 14*(3), 173-190.

STANGE, P. (1980). The sumarah movement in Javanese mysticism. (Doctoral dissertation, University of Wisconsin, Madison, Department of History, 1980).

WILEY, M. (1993). Silat seni gayong: Seven levels of self-defense. *Journal of Asian Martial Arts, 3*(4), 76-95.

chapter 5

Reflections on a Visit to the Shaolin Monastery

by Stanley E. Henning, M.A.

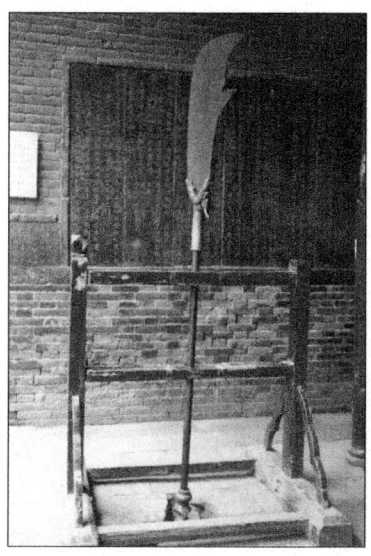

Above: A copy of Guan Gong's "Crescent Moon Halberd."
Page 64: Statue of Zhou Chang at Guanlin, Luoyang. According to tradition,
Zhou Chang was the halberd holder for Guan Gong.
All photographs courtesy of S. Henning.

I had studied some Chinese martial arts in Taiwan in the 1970's—taijiquan, sometimes referred to as "shadow boxing"; xingyiquan, a style of boxing that imitates animal movements; and some straight sword, curved broadsword, and spear routines. At the same time, I developed an interest in the history of the martial arts that, I must confess, has far surpassed my diligence in practicing these arts over the years. So, when I was invited to teach English in China in 1995, I also saw it as a wonderful opportunity to observe the current status of the martial arts there and continue on-site research into their origins and evolution.

The climax of my stay, anxiously awaited until the end of the school year, was a visit to the famed Shaolin Monastery, reputed home of gongfu. *Gongfu,* which in Chinese merely means "skill or effort expended to perfect a skill," was a term used by a French Jesuit P. M. Cibot in the 1770's to describe Daoist yoga-like exercises he had observed in China, but which, through usage outside China, now refers primarily to Chinese barehanded fighting (Needham, 1983: 170). In other words, gongfu is the inscrutable Westerner's term for what the Chinese merely call *quanshu* or "boxing," while the Chinese Mandarin term for "martial arts" is *wushu.*

Monkey, Pigsey, and Sandy attack a demon.
Taken from Li Zhuowu edition of *Journey to the West* (c. 1500).
Courtesy of Guggenheim Collection (microfilm).

My Shaolin odyssey began in Luoyang, an ancient capital of the Chinese empire for 960 years and home to numerous historical sites, including the Longmen Caves, which house a number of impressive Buddhist sculptures. The powerful guardian figures on either side of the entrances to the numerous grottoes attest to the fact that martial arts themes have, to varying degrees, permeated nearly every aspect of Chinese popular culture over the centuries. Then there is the Guanlin, or temple in memory of Guan Yunchang, also known as Guan Yu or Guan Gong, deified war hero of the Three Kingdoms period (220-265 C.E.), whose head is said to be enshrined there. On the left of the entrance to the main hall is a full size replica of the crescent moon halberd with which he reputedly fought his way to fame and the imaginations of generations of Chinese, Japanese and Koreans who have read of his exploits—a cross cultural symbol of East Asian tradition.

Up bright and early on the long awaited morning, I hopped aboard a minibus destined for the Shaolin Monastery. Fortunately I speak Mandarin, as I was the only non-Chinese aboard. After spending over half an hour roving the streets of Luoyang trying to fill the bus to capacity, our driver headed off for the Shaolin Monastery, over sixty kilometers to the southeast. Less than half way en route, we were diverted to a Taj Mahal-like roadside tourist "palace." The palace's dingy halls were filled with jerky mechanical figures depicting the legendary adventures in the novel, *Journey to the West,* of the Tang monk, Xuanzhuang, and his trusty companions Monkey, Pigsey and Sandy, to obtain the Buddhist scriptures in India. Before coming back out into the sunlight, I was forced to stand by with a mixture of impatience and amusement as I watched the members of my group delight in riding around on legless mechanized camels in a circle labeled "Thousand Mile Desert."

We ultimately arrived at our destination and, after twenty-six years of fascination with the Chinese martial arts, I was at last about to enter the world of the mystic, martial monks of Mount Song—the fount of many myths and, nowadays, as I was soon to discover, the source of much income from tourism. Filled with anticipation upon alighting from the minibus, I parted with my fellow Chinese passengers who had opted for a guided tour, and briskly made my way alone along the road leading to the monastery, passing martial arts supply stores and a number of gongfu schools.

The supply stores were filled to overflowing with weapons—staves, spears, swords, knives, halberds—everything imaginable for the total gongfu enthusiast. Most were imitations, suited only for demonstration. There were instances in history when even fight scenes in Chinese opera were enacted with real weapons, but those were the days when the martial arts were primarily life and death skills as opposed to "new age" vehicles for self-realization. During the Song dynasty (960-1279), these skills came to be called "The Eighteen Fighting Arts" after a list of eighteen of the most common weapons which a professional martial artist was expected to master. The lists varied, and sometimes included the matchlock. Boxing was usually at the end of the list in recognition of the fact that it was a basic skill, the foundation for all the traditional weapons—important, but not necessarily the weapon of choice as the gongfu movies would have one believe.

The gongfu schools in the vicinity of Shaolin Monastery began to sprout like "spring bamboo shoots after a rain" in the wake of the gongfu craze outside China in the late 1970's, which spread to China and reached high tide there following the worldwide showing of the movie "Shaolin Monastery" in the early 1980's. Poor families by the thousands pooled their meager savings to send their children to Shaolin training schools in hopes that the youngsters could become gongfu stars. The schools now take in foreigners as well, and one school in particular displays its new affluence through larger than life gongfu statues at its main entrance.

At one point, I stopped to marvel at a large, grotesque yellow-bellied "Happy Buddha," a grinning cement hulk announcing the entrance to the "Shaolin Amusement Palace," indicating that commercialism in its crassest form is now well ensconced on the slopes of Mount Song, central of China's five "sacred" mountains. Next, I came to the ticket booth. The entrance fee was quite steep by Chinese standards (forty yuan or five U.S. dollars), double the all day minibus fare. However, I was somewhat consoled by the fact that the fee was the same for both Chinese and *waibin*, which the Chinese insist means "foreign guest" but to the foreigner usually merely means "double price." Of course, the ticket was good for multiple sites and the ubiquitous cable car ride, assuming the cable car was operable.

On road to the Shaolin Monastery: the "Happy" Buddha entrance to "Shaolin Amusement Palace"; a martial arts paraphernalia shop. The characters above the entrance read "Knives and Swords."

Top, clockwise: (1) Shaolin Monastery in Emperor Kangxi's calligraphy (1662-1722) at the main entrance. (2) Figures purporting to show monks' martial arts training. Note "gecko" technique in background. (3-4) Modern larger than life figures in front of the Martial Arts Academy just outside the Shaolin Monastery precincts.

At last, my heart beat faster and visions of "Grasshopper," the mystic martial monk in the TV series "Kung Fu," flashed through my mind as I found myself actually approaching the main entrance to Shaolin Monastery, its name emblazoned above the entrance on a large, shiny black lacquered plaque with gold characters in the calligraphy of Emperor Kangxi (1662-1722).

Reverently stepping through the entrance into the compound, I noticed that, all along the central walkway, the old stone tablets were now interspersed with new ones, standing out like advertisements, representing foreign martial arts groups paying homage to the ostensible "home of gongfu."

A few moments later, I came upon the tablet erected in 728 C.E., the earliest historical record that alludes to the martial prowess of the monastery's residents (Tonami, 1990). It records one incident between 605-618 C.E. in which the monastery suffered considerable damage when the monks repulsed a group of marauders, and commemorates the role of thirteen of the monks in helping to capture one Wang Shichong, who had been a threat to the newly established Tang dynasty (618-907). Taking place in 621, this latter act saved the monastery from dissolution, the fate of other monasteries in the area at the time. The tablet was erected primarily to consolidate the monastery's claims to property ceded as a reward for the monks' assistance. One of the monks, Tanzong, was given the title "Great General," but there is no mention whatsoever of the monks' martial arts skills. While they likely had such skills, they were even more likely picked because of their leadership abilities in marshaling a local makeshift militia in response to Imperial decree.

For about nine hundred years following these exploits, there is no record of Shaolin Monastery's association with martial arts, even during the Song (960-1279), while monks at Mount Wutai, Shanxi Province, and other locations were sacrificing themselves defending against Jin invaders (Li, 1974: 254, n. 17).

Following the crowd, I then entered a newly arranged courtyard containing a ring for staging demonstrations surrounded by a series of cubicles filled with life-size figures depicting the monks' involvement in the martial arts. One cubicle showing a monk scaling a wall with his "gecko skills" was a particular challenge to credibility. The real priorities of monastic life centered around study, lectures, meditation, and hard work, especially for the young acolytes, in the kitchen, around the grounds and in the fields.

Martial arts practice was more like a diversion for a relatively small percentage of the monks who had brought these skills with them into the monastery and a few who could find time to learn from them to help defend the monastery. The reality was a far cry from the pulp fiction accounts that describe a highly organized martial arts training program culminating in an initiation by running a gauntlet of cleverly constructed dummies.

The number and quality of the resident martial artists varied considerably over the centuries. During the last half of the sixteenth century, the monastery's martial arts "high tide," a number of visitors recorded their observations in poems. From these descriptions, the monks appear to have practiced the known styles of the day. One observer specifically describes a lively demonstration of "monkey boxing"; however, there was apparently no such thing as a unique Shaolin style of boxing. To that time, only a form of staff fighting had been named for the monastery. Ming general, Yu Dayou (1503-1580), disappointed with what he saw, selected a couple of young monks to accompany him in the field during anti-pirate operations, receive on-the-job training, and return to raise the standards of their compatriots' staff fighting skills. On the other hand, a number of monks acquitted themselves well enough in these same anti-pirate campaigns to be immortalized as "Shaolin Monk Soldiers" and perpetuate the monastery's legendary fame. A few are among the over two hundred prominent former residents memorialized in the nearby graveyard known as the Forest of Stupas.

"Iron Staff Li, Beginning Form" (Drunken Step and Monkey Boxing both evolve from this). Taken from Zhang Kongzhao's *Boxing Classics: Essential of Boxing* (c. 1784), 1900 edition. Courtesy of Taiwan Academia Sinica, Institute for History and Philology, Fu Sinian Library.

In 1659, nearly two decades after the beginning of Manchu (Qing) rule, an observer noted that the monastery was in a state of disrepair and inhabited by only one or two tattered old monks who ordered young acolytes to demonstrate "boxing and staff" just like little street beggars (Wang, 1659). In 1828, Manchu official Lin Qing (1791-1846) visited the monastery and was treated to a boxing demonstration which he described in terms from the Daoist classic, *Zhuangzi*, as agile like a bird and powerful as a bear. In 1936, a foreign visitor described the place as isolated and empty with no living trace of the martial arts, a far cry from the present carnival-like atmosphere generated by thousands of tourists, both domestic and foreign. Clearly, the monastery's fortune has waxed and waned with the currents of human affairs (Hers, 1936: 76-82).

The monastery's fame has led to the name "Shaolin" being appended to numerous martial arts styles and even the myth that Chinese boxing originated there. Famous historian and Ming patriot Huang Zongxi (1610-1695) was at least partially responsible for this misperception. For the first time, Huang's *Epitaph to Wang Zhengnan* (c. 1669) described boxing as originally comprising an aggressive Shaolin "external" style which could be easily overcome by a yielding "internal" style originated during the Song dynasty by a Daoist alchemist, Zhang Sanfeng, who was said to have resided on Mount Wudang in Hubei province. In view of Huang's prominent role in southern Ming resistance to Qing rule, the epitaph, filled as it is with possible anti-Qing symbolism (the External Shaolin School representing the Manchus and the Internal School the Chinese), appears to have been meant more as a political jab at the foreign conquerors than as boxing history when it was written. However, the *Epitaph* was widely accepted as gospel and still dominates the Chinese view of their martial arts.

Forrest of Stupas — The Shaolin Monastery's graveyard.

Ming period writings on the subject by Tang Shunzhi (1507-1560), Qi Jiguang (1528-1587), He Liangchen (c. 1591), and Zheng Ruozeng (1505-1580) all fail to mention Shaolin boxing among their lists of well-known styles of the day. Cheng Zongyou (1561-?), who claims to have spent ten years in the monastery studying staff fighting, explains that, during his stay, the monks were emphasizing boxing to try to bring this skill up to the same level as the famed Shaolin Staff; however, Cheng offers no description of the content of their boxing.

Zhang Kongzhao's boxing manual, *Boxing Classic: Essentials of Boxing* (c. 1784), which purports to record the teachings of a Shaolin monk, Xuanji, is primarily a discourse on basic principles which might easily apply to boxing in general. It does describe some forms associated with Monkey Boxing and Drunken Eight Immortals, as well as some mentioned in General Qi Jiguang's *Boxing Classic* (c. 1561), in the overall context of what it calls Shaolin Monastery Short Hitting technique. The principles enumerated in this manual are in accord with other Ming period writings on martial arts, including Cheng Zongyou's staff manual, revealing that Shaolin martial arts mirrored those practiced in the society at large.

During the early 1800's, secret society members sought to associate themselves with the monastery's Ming period patriotic image. They fabricated a "history" which traced their lineage to a mythical group of Shaolin monks whom they claimed had assisted Emperor Kangxi defeat a group of would-be invaders. They claimed these patriotic monks were then betrayed by court intriguers and forced to flee south to Fujian Province, where they were said to have established a second Shaolin Monastery which was, in turn, allegedly destroyed as a result of further treachery. According to the myth, the survivors of all this became the six progenitors of the Heaven and Earth Society (originally established in Fujian around 1769), also known as the Triads or Hong League.

By the end of the nineteenth century, proponents of so-called southern styles of boxing, many of whom were likely secret society members, began to claim southern Shaolin Monastery origins for their martial arts. One of these styles, Hongquan, which includes the Five Animal forms often associated with Shaolin boxing, was said to have been passed down by a man named Hong Xiguan. The problem with this was that Hong was not a real person but merely a character in a popular chivalric novel, *Emperor Qianlong Visits Jiangnan* (south of the Yangzi River) (c. 1893-96). Yet another style, Mojiaquan, was said to have originated with the Fujian Shaolin monk, Zhishan Chanshi (Zen

Master), another character out of the same novel.

Similar spurious information appeared on the eve of the 1911 Revolution in a secret society inspired boxing manual that was later published as *Secrets of Shaolin Boxing* (1915) under the patriotic pseudonym, Master of the Studio of Self-Respect. To this day, much of the misinformation, both inside and outside of China surrounding the origins and evolution of Shaolin boxing, can be traced to this book.

Next, I came to the large, impressive Thousand Buddha Hall with its lively wall murals of the five hundred Luohan or disciples of Buddha. Looking down for a moment, I gazed upon the forty-eight concave impressions in the stone floor said to have been caused by monks practicing basic martial arts stances and movements. However, this was an assumption which was not totally convincing, because such a phenomenon is not necessarily unusual when stone or brick is laid over a plain earthen bed. In other words, the impressions might just as well have been caused by monks participating in scripture chanting activities over a long period of time. In any case, this was the biggest mystery I encountered at the monastery.

The unequivocal highlight of my visit was White Robe Hall, popularly called "Boxing Manual Hall" for its animated Qing Period (1644-1911) wall murals depicting boxing and weapons practice as well as historical and legendary incidents involving the monastery. One of the murals depicts an incident said to have taken place at the end of the Yuan Dynasty (1271-1368). It is the legend of a monk who, transforming himself into a fierce giant brandishing a flaming staff, supposedly scared off a band of marauding Red Turban rebels and saved the monastery. What visitors are not told is the fact discretely ignored by Shaolin monks over the centuries that the monastery was actually overrun at the end of the Yuan, half its buildings destroyed, and its residents scattered to other locations until it was safe to return—perhaps one of the most successful cover-ups in history (Xu and Xu: 100)! Despite this inglorious episode, the facts were "forgotten," the legend enshrined, and a form of staff fighting was named for the monastery—a miraculous recovery from ignominy.

Cheng Zongyou memorializes the monastery's legendary savior, known as King Jinnaluo, with an illustration in the preface to his manual, *Elucidation of Shaolin Staff Methods* (1621). According to monastery records, Shaolin alone had King Jinnaluo as its guardian saint, while Guan Yu was given this role in other Chinese Buddhist monasteries. Apparently widely known at the time, this story probably served a dual purpose: to warn away would-be intruders as well as remind the residents of their responsibility to defend the monastery. A hall was dedicated to King Jinnaluo but it, along with many other buildings, was destroyed as a result of warlord activities in 1928.

The two old murals at each end of the hall, one depicting boxing and the other weapons practice, tie in Shaolin Monastery's past with its present, confirming the fact that martial arts were indeed practiced here yet unwittingly negating the myth that they were necessarily part of a weaponless religious discipline.

"Divine image of the appearance of the great saint King Jinnaluo," taken from Cheng Zongyou's *Elucidation of Shaolin Staff Methods* (c. 1621). Courtesy of National Central Library, Taipei, Taiwan.

That the monastery's residents were not even always what they appeared to be is revealed in the observations of Wang Shixing (1546-1598). Wang comments that Henan monks acted as they pleased, never taking the diploma of their order, shaving their heads and becoming monks one day, and growing their hair long and becoming common citizens the next. In troubled times, members of the White Lotus Sect members would enter the monastery in large numbers to escape scrutiny by the authorities until the coast was clear (Wang, 1936: 9). So, among the so-called monks in the monastery, there was only one in a hundred who didn't drink or eat meat and all they knew was the "fist and staff" of the martial arts as opposed to the "stick and shout" of Chan (Zen) Buddhism (Wang, 1981: 41).

Guardian figures at Longmen, Luoyang.

Mural in the White Robe Hall showing boxing practice in
the Shaolin Monastery. Painted in the late Qing Dynasty.

The murals provide a timeless image of past performances and those now being staged in the courtyard near the monastery entrance and in the numerous martial arts schools in the vicinity. While solo practice familiarizes the martial artist with specific techniques and serves as a mnemonic device in tying them together, the heart of training lies in duo sets as depicted in the murals: groups of two protagonists pitted against each other, one lets fly a punch or a kick and the other blocks, seizes or dodges, each alternating attack or defense in rapid succession. Double curved broadswords whirl about their wielder—one parries the thrust of a spear while the other lunges at the spearman, the spear withdraws with a twist, deflecting the broadsword—I stand transfixed as the murals appear to come alive for one brief moment before I turn to leave.

After wandering through the Forest of Stupas outside the monastery, I was ready to make the climb to Bodhidharma Cave, where the legendary patriarch of Chan Buddhism is said to have sat meditating for nine years (c. 525-534), projecting his image into a stone in front of him as if the stone were a computer screen without a screen saver; however, glancing at my watch, I realized that time was running out and I had to get back to the minibus. I didn't feel too disappointed though, since I already knew that Bodhidharma didn't have anything to do with Chinese martial arts (Spiessbach, 1992). The widespread misperception that long-standing Chinese tradition attributes the origins of Chinese boxing to Bodhidharma is contradicted by the fact that this myth first appeared only around 1907 in the popular novel, *Travels of Lao Can*, by Liu Tieyun (1986: 73, 248 n. 4). Furthermore, the popular notion that the Chinese martial arts were somehow influenced by Chan Buddhism appears to be based on a combination of this and other secret society myths, the fact that martial arts really were practiced in Shaolin Monastery, and viewing the Chinese martial arts through Japanese eyes or misassociating certain Japanese Zen/samurai swordsmanship concepts with the Chinese martial arts.

As the minibus headed back to Luoyang, I began to reflect on the day's experience and the significance of Shaolin Monastery in Chinese martial arts history. The temple in honor of the warrior hero, Guan Yu, reminded me that the Chinese martial arts were widespread throughout the popular culture. Reference to the existence of a six-chapter boxing manual in the history of the Former Han dynasty (206 BC-24 C.E.) is also an indication that Chinese boxing was probably already quite sophisticated by that time. As perhaps the most widely practiced indigenous form of physical culture at the time, it was only natural that these skills would be introduced into monasteries with the spread of Buddhism in China, and that they would be reflected in art as witnessed by the guardian statues at the Longmen grottoes. Even the characters in the popular novel, *Journey to the West,* were martial artists, Monkey with his magic staff and Pigsey with his rake. Shaolin Monastery, located in the geomantic center of ancient Chinese civilization, and continually subject to the ebb and flow of events as recorded with a mix of fact and fancy, has served as a mirror of Chinese popular culture and a symbol of the martial arts.

REFERENCES

HENNING, S. (1981). The Chinese martial arts in historical perspective. *Military Affairs* [now *Journal of Military History*], 45(4), 173-178.

HENNING, S. (1995). On politically correct treatment of myths in the Chinese martial arts. *The Chenstyle Journal*, 3(2), 17-21.

HENNING, S. (1997). Chinese boxing: The internal versus external schools in the light of history and theory. *Journal of Asian Martial Arts*, 6(3), 10-19.

HERS, J. (1936). The sacred mountains of China: Song Shan, the deserted. *The China Journal*, 24(2), 76-82.

HUANG, R. (1981). *The year of no significance: The Ming dynasty in decline.* New Haven: Yale University Press.

LI, C. (Trans.), (1974). *The travel diaries of Hsu Hsia-k'o.* Hong Kong: Chinese University of Hong Kong.

LIU, T. (1986). *The travels of Lao T'san.* (Reprint). (H. Shadick, Trans.). Westport: Greenwood Press.

MURRY, D., AND QIN, B. (1994). *The origins of the tiandihui: The Chinese Triads in legend and history.* Stanford: Stanford University Press.

NEEDHAM, J. (1983). *Science and civilization in China, Vol. 5,* Part V. Cambridge: Cambridge University Press.

SPIESSBACH, M. (1992). Bodhidharma: Meditating monk, martial arts master or make-believe? *Journal of Asian Martial Arts*, 1(4), 10-27.

TONAMI, M. (1990). *The Shaolin monastery stele on Mount Song.* (P. Herbert, Trans.). Kyoto: Italian School of East Asian Studies.

WANG, J. (Ed.), (1659). *Zhongzhou miscellany.* Juan 75, Shaolin Staff. Hand copied manuscript on microfilm.

WANG, S. (1936). *Henan annals.* Shanghai: Shangwu.

WANG, S. (1981). *Record of wide-ranging travels,* juan 3. Beijing: Zhonghua.

XU, J. AND XU, G. (Eds.). (1995). *Henan-Luoyang history.* Zhengzhou: Zhongzhou Guji Chubanshe.

chapter 6

Reviving the Daoist Roots of Internal Martial Arts

by Mark Hawthorne

Monk of the orthodox Complete Reality Sect. Photograph by Kipling Swehla.
Photos courtesy of the Taoist Restoration Society.

When Zhang Sanfeng began developing taijiquan as a comprehensive system of martial arts in the thirteenth century, this Daoist monk ensured his place in history as the first patriarch of the art. Of course, history can get muddled with the passing centuries, but Zhang is generally credited with synthesizing the philosophical principles of Daoism with a martial art that could be used for both self-defense and a method to enhance one's internal energy (*qi*). Thus, Daoist monks used taijiquan to defend themselves and as an exercise for the mind and body (Liang, 1996: 8-9).

Seven centuries later, taijiquan is still a popular martial art, both in China and around the world. But while the art has flowered into a global practice, its roots have been nearly destroyed, and Daoism exists only as a fragile remnant of the past or more a vestigial tradition than the vigorous philosophy and religion that was once one of China's most important belief systems. Whether or not Daoism can be revived may well depend on the efforts of those in China now struggling to rebuild the monasteries and temples and to bring back the clergy who once populated them.

The threat to Daoism began in the last century as the power of the Qing Dynasty (1644-1912) began to decline. As China became weak enough to be invaded by Western powers, many suspected the Daoists of plotting against the emperor, and imperial support began to drop. China finally shed its imperial dynasties and founded a Nationalist Government in 1912; gone were the powerful emperors who had long supported the Daoist monasteries and temples. The new government, which believed Daoism to be based on the superstition and folklore, allowed the system to struggle on its own, and monasteries and temples fell into disrepair.

Photography by Kipling Swehla.

In 1949, Mao Zedong and his Communists toppled China's government and then outlawed Daoism altogether. They reasoned that an ideologically perfect state made religion unnecessary. Monasteries were destroyed or requisitioned as government buildings, and monks, nuns and Daoist officials were imprisoned in labor camps, reducing the clergy from several millions to about 50,000.

Today there is a new mind-set in China, a more liberal attitude that sees religious expression as an important part of traditional Chinese culture and a direct link to such martial arts as xingyiquan and taijiquan. Daoist sites must be restored, say supporters of this ancient tradition, and the clergy must be allowed to transmit their mystic teachings to the next generation. And thus the race to save Daoism, China's oldest indigenous religion, is on.

One group leading the work to rescue Daoism is the Taoist Restoration Society (TRS) (Taoist, 1999). Brock Silvers founded the nonprofit organization nine years ago after visiting China and seeing for himself how Daoism was threatened with extinction. "By the early 1980's," he says, "most Western scholars believed that Daoism had been effectively stamped out by China's modern upheavals. We thought Daoism was a dead religion" (personal communication, 1999).

Although based in the U.S., the TRS works out of Beijing to support the restoration of monastic institutions and assist Daoist communities. The organization works to rebuild Daoist sites for their original purpose, not as museums or tourist attractions. It also supports the revival of organized Daoism and is especially involved in the restoration of temples, almost all of which—some where in the tens of thousands—were requisitioned or destroyed by the government.

The Chinese leadership has joined the effort with its own organization, the National Daoist Association (NOA), which officially oversees all Daoist activity in China. Headquartered in Beijing, the NDA runs the entire national Daoist organization. Its new director is Min Zhiting, a well-respected Daoist monk. These two groups, combined with the work of Daoist monks, nuns and other supporters, are working within what Silvers sees as a "ten year window of opportunity to save Daoism" (personal communication, 1999).

Dao of Daoism

Nature is the model that Daoists use as a guide for ideal behavior, including the practice of martial arts. By observing nature, we see that everything is in balance and governed by the same laws. By imitating nature, we learn to both survive and live in harmony. Hua Tuo (141-203 C.E.), a Chinese physician, introduced a system of renewing one's qi with a combination of mental, physical and breathing exercises called *daoyin*. He also created a system of exercises known as the Sport of the Five Animals, which seeks to imitate the speed, agility and power of such animals as the bear, crane, deer, monkey and tiger. From these exercises came Hua's Five Animal Games, regarded as the first system of martial arts in China (Breslow, 1995: 192-195).

Photography: left by Brock Silvers, and right by Katherine McVety.

Daoism refers to both a philosophy (*daojia*) and a religion (*daojiao*) and is thought to have developed in China in the sixth and fifth centuries B.C.E. As a philosophy, Daoism stresses that one should not try to change the way things are—nature provides everything. Religious Daoism evolved from several philosophical and religious movements, and the first temple was founded in the second century C.E. Religious Daoism incorporates the worship of many gods and a veneration of nature and simplicity. Because Daoists view the body and spirit as one, the goal is not to liberate the soul from the body but to nurture one's qi and attain the Dao by realizing the truth within you (Schumacher, 1996: 162-173).

Dao ("the Way") plays an important role in both religious and philosophical Daoism. It is concerned with the course of events and order of the universe. It is an intangible reality that gives rise to existence. All things, in time, return to the Dao. Dao may also be understood as "the Way things do what they do." There is a Way to do everything, and once you master that, you need not be concerned with it. For example, after learning the Way to ride a bicycle, the rider doesn't have to think about it; he simply does it. Practitioners of Daoism attempt to gain mystical union with the Dao through meditation and by following the nature of the Dao in thought and action (Schumacher, 1996: 163-166).

The Dao is a principal feature of two classic Daoist texts, the *Daodejing* (The Book of the Way and Its Power) and the *Zhuangzi*. Many scholars credit authorship of the *Daodejing* to Laozi, the Chinese philosopher believed to have lived in the the sixth century B.C.E. Although the book's origin is in debate, it forms the basis of both religious and philosophical Daoism.

The Daoist sage Zhuangzi (c. 369-286 B.C.E.) is regarded as the author of the text by the same name. The Zhuangzi's views on Dao, *de* ("power") and *wuwei* ("non-doing" or "inaction") mirror those of the *Daodejing* (Schumacher, 1996: 210-211).

Wuwei is an important tenet in martial arts. Inaction finds its power within the individual and his understanding of the nature of all things. It is a natural law for all things to always be what they are—interfere with this law and you have failed. Challenges are to be ignored, says the *Daodejing*, and wuwei is the only means of achieving true success (Barrett, 1993: 28). Compare these principles with the efficacy of redirecting an opponent's attack, allowing him to be thrown off-guard and conquered by his own inertia.

Yin-yang is another central aspect of Daoism. These two contradictory yet complementary energies are said to be the cause of the universe and represent the duality of existence. Yin and yang are manifestations of the Dao of the supreme ultimate, or the Supreme One, which is known in Chinese as *taiji* (taijiquan translates as the "fist of the supreme ultimate"). Yin is feminine, receptive and soft. Yang is masculine, creative and hard. While yin symbolizes the moon, shadows, death and earth, yang represents the sky, light, life and fire. These two polarities are in constant fluctuation, with one side dominating and then yielding to the other. Nothing is ever purely yin or yang; all things are comprised of varying degrees of both. A cloud, for example, might be yin because it is soft and yang because it is white (Schumacher, 1996: 216-219).

Photography by Kipling Swehla.

Dao of Martial Arts

Although taijiquan might seem the most obvious connection, the Daoist tenets of yielding and softness have given birth to other martial arts, especially the "internal" styles. In Daoist spiritual training the internal martial arts are used for both spiritual development and external power. The four internal styles are bagua, xingyiquan, liuhebafa and taijiquan (Wong, 1997: 226).

"The differences between external and internal martial arts do not arise from specific techniques employed by the various styles," says Wai Lun Choi, who teaches internal martial arts in Chicago, Illinois. "The differences stem from the way the movements are produced. External styles emphasize speed and power, but this is also true of the internal arts. What really differentiates them are the training methods used to develop this speed and power. Internal styles require a precise unity of breathing, weight distribution, joint alignment, leverage, etc., any time a movement is executed" (personal communication, 1999).

Bagua ("Eight Trigrams," refers to heaven, earth, water, fire, thunder, wind, mountain and lake) most likely grew from Daoism in the seventeenth century into a variety of systems practiced around the world today. The bagua boxing style uses fluid motions and swift footwork, moving in circles to confuse the opponent. The victor outflanks his rival, remaining safely behind or beside the source of danger. Bagua demands exceptional concentration (Wong, 1997: 226-227).

Photography by Kipling Swehla.

Xingyiquan ("Form and Intention Fist") is attributed to Yue Fei, a twelfth century Chinese general. Although he helped popularize it, Yue credited a wandering Daoist with teaching him the art. As with many legends, its accuracy is questionable (others date the art to the Shaolin Temple in the sixth century), but xingyiquan remains very martial in appearance, characterized by pounding, thrusting and hitting with bursts of movement. Xingyiquan is efficient in its expression of power, with the practitioner using a full range of body motions for grappling, locking, throwing and trapping techniques (Wong, 1997: 227).

Liuhebafa ("Six Harmonies and Eight Methods") is probably the least known of the internal martial arts, at least in the West. This art blends elements of taiji, bagua and xingyiquan. "Unlike the other three internal arts," says Wai Lun Choi, "liuhebafa uses over 700 different techniques. The art rests on a foundation of biology, physiology and anatomy, and the spirit enables its proper performance. Its theory, from every perspective, complies with what is practical and scientifically sound. To develop yourself, you must turn away from mysticism and the belief in secrets you imagine will transform you. Science and nature are your true teachers and correct training is what will transform you" (personal communication, 1999).

Taijiquan, perhaps the most popular of the internal arts founded on Daoism, is a subtle system practiced today primarily for its health benefits. The style, which seeks to cultivate one's qi, finds maximum efficiency through integrating the mind and body in harmonious movement. *Qi* is described as that through which the Dao manifests itself and then differentiates into two forces—yin and yang. Taijiquan practitioners use the doctrine of yin and yang throughout their training. In push-hands practice, for example, it is only by achieving softness and yielding to the opponent's attack that he is effectively repelled (Kauz, 1997: 60). "Most of the traditional internal martial arts training is still underground in China and was so long before Mao," says Dr. Yang Jwing-Ming, author and martial arts instructor for more than thirty years. "These arts have been considered top secret since ancient times when they were taught mainly in the monasteries. Even then, they were taught with the goal of spiritual enlightenment." All that changed in 1911. "Beginning in the late Qing Dynasty, and continuing for some time afterward, the knowledge of internal martial arts was gradually revealed to people outside the monastic community. But then the Communist party took over and they started to control the martial arts community and kept the real martial arts suppressed, fearing the martial artists would unite against the party rule. Combat techniques in martial arts training have been gradually neglected in China ever since" (personal communication, 1999).

Photography by Kipling Swehla.

Dr. Yang, who was raised in Taiwan and has lived in the U.S. for 25 years, believes there is only one way to keep the internal martial arts alive. "I visited mainland China recently," he says, "and I was surprised to learn that no one under fifty even understands the relationship between qi and the *jin*—that is, internal power. There is still some traditional training in the Chinese countryside, but only a small number of traditional practitioners. I realized the only way to preserve the internal arts was to teach them outside of China" (personal communication, 1999).

Although Daoism's link to external martial arts is more difficult to establish, a case can be made that many of these arts are indebted to the central Daoist principle of the duality of opposites. Indeed, probably any style that advocates fluid motion, yielding responses and avoiding or redirecting an opponent's attack can claim Daoism as its inspiration. As the *Daodejing* says:

> Rushing into action, you fail.
> Trying to grasp things, you lose them.
> Forcing a project to completion,
> You ruin what was almost ripe.
> - Mitchell, 1991: 64

Daoism Today

TRS and NDA would like to ensure that every major city in China has at least one major Daoist place of worship. Although there is no official restoration plan, major Daoist sites have been the first to be renovated, a task that often involves a construction company. Smaller projects are usually handled by Daoist clergy, often with the assistance of volunteers from the lay community. While the government pays for its own projects, funds for much of the other reconstruction come from supporters throughout Asia, Europe and the United States. The final cost of a restoration varies widely: anywhere from a few hundred U.S. dollars to several million, depending on the size of the site and extent of damage.

Silvers notes that it is difficult to control the use of Daoist iconography and symbols. "From what I have seen," he says, "the government doesn't really care about authenticity. And even those who do care—officials and monks alike—are often hampered by a combination of poverty and ignorance" (personal communication, 1999). Which is why TRS not only helps fund projects, but puts pressure on the Chinese government to use greater care as sites are being rebuilt.

The government's National Daoist Association and local religious affairs bureaus across China are also working to save the tradition from extinction, with varying degrees of success. Last January, for example, the government opened a renovated temple dedicated to the god of Tai Shan. The ancient temple, one of the largest in Beijing, was a favorite of the Qing emperors and was rebuilt by a local tourist bureau. Thus, rather than being renovated as a place of worship, the temple now stands as a cultural museum and no Daoist clergy are allowed to engage in religious activity there.

Photography: left by Kipling Swehla, and right by Katherine McVety.

Daoism Tomorrow

With so many people working on national and local levels toward a goal that is paramount to preserving China's culture, it is tempting to believe that the fight to save Daoism is won. After all, if it's something everyone wants, why the struggle? But turning the tide on a century of destruction is not a simple matter.

The good news is that the restoration of Daoism seems to be taking hold, with major temples crowded on holidays, new sites being constructed and the quality of renovations constantly improving. People throughout China have been very receptive to their reborn Daoist traditions, with more and more viewing themselves as Daoist. But it will take more than renovated temples and contented practitioners to ensure Daoism's survival. As Silvers explains:

> The real window of opportunity involves the expected life spans of the old, pre-Communist generation of clergy—the *laodao* masters—who are generally seventy to one hundred years old. With each temple that is restored or reactivated, more laodao are recalled from the fields, the retired workers' hospitals or any kind of work unit to which they might have been assigned.
>
> Although these laodao are not numerous, they have embraced the task of breeding a new generation of religious seekers and leaders. It is imperative that organized Daoism reclaims its heritage before the current supply of laodao passes away. When these adepts pass away, the previous Daoist age will go with them (personal communication, 1999).

These *laodao* (elder Daoists) include China's many martial arts masters, whose teachings were suppressed under the threat of imprisonment and death during Mao's reign. The progressive decline of China's traditional martial arts is also a loss to the world, where the destruction of any cultural expression is disgraceful.

Adds Silvers (personal communication, 1999): "It would certainly be a tragedy to witness the functional extinction of the tradition which gave so much impetus and energy to the early development of the internal martial arts. The internal arts and Daoism will forever be linked; can one really be whole without the other?"

Mindful that Chinese President Jiang Zemin already has his hands full, Silvers remains hopeful. "Things are already so much better than they were ten or twenty years ago," he says. "Average Han Chinese people do have more religious freedom than their parents did. And the human soul abhors a vacuum. But traditions and places and rituals and songs and prayers and the like are being forgotten every day. Half a religion probably can't survive. But we might succeed yet" (personal communication, 1999).

Photography by Kipling Swehla.

REFERENCES

BARRETT, T. (1993). *Dao: To know and not be knowing.* San Francisco, CA: Chronicle Books.

BRESLOW, A. (199 5). *Beyond the closed door: Chinese culture and the creation of t'ai chi ch'uan.* Jerusalem, Israel: Almond Blossom Press.

CHUANG-TZU. (1998). *The essential Chuang-Tzu.* (S. Hamill and J. Seaton, Trans.). Boston, MA: Shambala Publications.

FRANTIZ , B. (1998). *The power of internal martial arts: Combat secrets of ba gua, tai chi and hsing-i.* Berkeley, CA: North Atlantic Books.

KAUZ, H. (1997). *Push hands: The handbook for noncompetitive tai chi practice with a partner.* Woodstock, NY: The Overlook Press.

LIANG, S. (1996). *Tai chi chuan.* Rosindale, MA: YMAA Publication Center.

MITCHELL, S. (1991). *Tao te ching.* New York, NY: HarperPerennial.

SCHUMACHER, S., AND WOERNER, G. (1996). *Shambala dictionary of Daoism.* Boston, MA: Shambala Publications.

TAOIST RESTORATION SOCIETY (1999). http://www.taorestore.com.

WONG, E. (1997). *The Shambala guide to Daoism.* Boston, MA: Shambala Publications.

chapter 7

Asceticism and the Pursuit of Death by Warriors and Monks

by Ken Jeremiah, M.A.

"Tomorrow I will be buried alive. I wonder how long I will survive, without water and in complete darkness. Two or three days perhaps..."

Introduction

There has long been a connection between the martial and the spiritual paths in Japan. Martial artists strive to understand *ki* (Chinese, *qi*), the universal energy that permeates all things, and the true source of a warrior's speed and strength. The body and mind have limitations. The energy of the universe does not. In order to understand and utilize this energy for practical purposes, advanced students of the martial arts engage in meditation and other spiritual exercises. In so doing, they immerse themselves in exercises originally developed for religious practices. Such practices and corresponding beliefs intermingle with the physical techniques of their respective arts so completely that it is sometimes difficult to separate the two.

Some arts, like Yagyu Shinkage Ryu, founded by Yagyu Munenori (1571-1646), and Niten Ichi Ryu, which claims descent from Miyamoto Musashi (c. 1584-1645), have been heavily influenced by Zen Buddhism. Other arts, such as Kashima Shinto Ryu, formulated by Bokuden Tsukahara (1489-1571), and Aikido,[1] founded by Ueshiba Morihei (1883-1969), are based on Shinto beliefs.

The spiritual training that exists in different martial arts originated for practical, military reasons. It is necessary for the warrior to eliminate fear. "Fear distracts, destroying concentration, reactions and timing. Technical virtuosity with weapons is useless to a warrior that cannot control his fear—as in the familiar case of athletes who perform flawlessly in practice but are unable to function in important competitions. Ultimate proficiency in deadly combat, then, requires the ability to set aside fear—to maintain a kind of detachment from the possible consequences of the activity" (Friday, 1997: 15).

If a martial artist is afraid of death and concerned with the outcome of a bout, he cannot perform his art with complete freedom, and he cannot completely integrate the art into his own life. So, it is necessary to develop a frame of mind that embraces death as something that should not be feared. Death should be thought of as simply a part of life (Sugawara, 1988: 140).

After the Warring States Era[2] had ended, there was a long, sustained period of peace in Japan. Warriors, looking to attain a state of mind that has no fear of anything, including death, turned to *shugyo* (ascetic discipline). Shugyo training methods include extremely enduring and possibly life-threatening practices, such as extended periods of starvation, immersion in freezing waters, and secluding oneself in deep caves for weeks on end in meditation, aspiring to eliminate the boundary separating life and death, so that life and death can be perceived for what they are: different facets of the same phenomenon. Just as *yin* and *yang* (Jp. *in* and *yo*) cannot exist independently of one another, without death there could be no life, and without life, death would not exist. Takamura Yukiyoshi, headmaster of the Takamura Branch of Shindo Yoshin Ryu, explains the purpose of such ascetic practices: "The heart and mind must wrestle with demons and be victorious to find enlightenment. Without a struggle, the character is never challenged and never matures. That is why shugyo is so important" (Takamura, 1999: 30).

The *yamabushi*, also known as *shugenja*, took such training to extremes. There is one training method called "weighing of karma," in which an individual hangs his body head-first over the edge of a precipice, and another puts some pressure on his legs to keep him from falling to his death (Hitoshi, 2001: 123). Another similar practice again involves suspending an individual head-first over the edge of a cliff, but with ropes. At the end of the training session, when others are hauling the trainee back to the top, they release their grip on the ropes for a moment, making the initiate believe that he is plummeting to his death (Friday, 1997: 16).

Although such practices may sound extreme, some yamabushi actually went further. Some eliminated the separation of life and death and lived for their deaths alone. They intentionally died, so that they might live forever. This is the relatively unknown practice of self-mummification, the act of becoming a Buddha in this very body.

A Living Buddha

In the year 1783, Daijuku Bosatsu Shinnyokai Shonin decided to commit himself alive to the earth. His death was a long and painful one, taking about ten years to accomplish. He spent approximately three years consuming nothing but twigs and berries. This eliminated fat deposits on the body, which easily decompose after death. During the next 1,000 days, he ate pine bark and resin, which function as a preservative. For the final 1,000-day period, he drank tea made from *urushi*, a toxic substance that was used to make lacquer. The accumulation of toxins within the body protected it from desecration by insects or animals after death.

After enduring such harsh, self-inflicted treatment for nearly a decade, the monk was buried alive. He sat in a stone room, in complete darkness, and meditated until his death. A breathing tube was in place to provide oxygen as long as he rang a bell daily. Once the bell stopped ringing, the tube was removed and the tomb sealed. Three years later, the tomb was opened. His body had mummified, and he became a *sokushinbutsu*: a living Buddha.

Mummification can be either accidental or intentional. In ancient Egypt, bodies were mummified for postmortem religious beliefs. The Egyptians believed that two human spiritual essences passed to the afterlife, the *ba* (character/personality) and the *ka* (soul/life-force). "For a person to make the voyage into the next world, his *ba* and *ka* must be able to reunite in his body. For this to happen, the physical body of the deceased must be preserved in as recognizable a form as possible" (David and Archbold, 2000: 67).

During the embalming process, which took approximately seventy days, after all liquids had been drained from the body, the brain and the internal organs were removed, preventing decay. Then, the body was stuffed with a type of salt called natron. After forty days, the natron was removed and the body covered with linen that had been soaked in scented oil. This was not simply a means of disposing of the deceased. Rather, it was a necessary step in immortalizing the person.

Similar mummification procedures were found in other societies, including Chinese, Incan, and Alaskan Aleutian cultures (Small, 2004: 10). There is evidence that important people were mummified before cremation in ancient India, and in China, many Chan (Jp. *Zen*) priests were mummified after death and enshrined in temples as objects of worship. This practice began in the Jin Dynasty (266-316 C.E.) and has continued to the present day. "The most recent case may be that of [Shi Cihang], a native of [Fujian], who died in Taiwan in 1955 and was mummified four years later" (Sharf, 1992: 2). Even today, mummification of human corpses continues. Gunther von Hagens, the designer of Body Worlds, has made over 200 million dollars by displaying the mummified, skinless remains of human beings. Over twenty million people have gone to see the corpses, and China is currently taking action to stop the illegal mummification and trafficking of human corpses (Barboza, 2006).

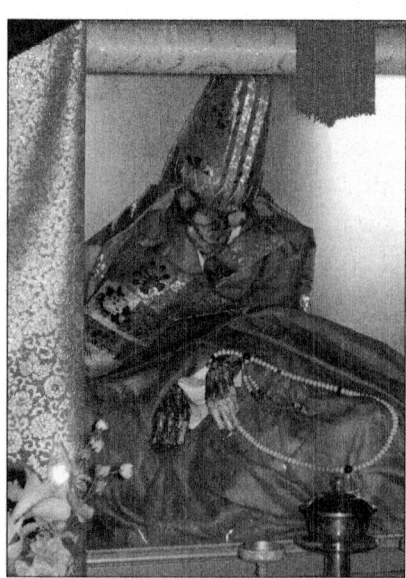

The body of Daijuku Bosatsu Shinnyokai Shonin on
display at Dainichibo Temple in Yamagata, Japan.
Photograph courtesy of Ken Jeremiah.

Accidental mummifications also occur. Mummifications that are classified as class one, or simple, "signify that there has been no human attempt to preserve the body tissues, and the preservation occurred secondarily to climatic conditions. This form of preservation has been documented for most New World mummies. The decomposition of soft tissue is influenced by both internal and external factors, and is accelerated by warm and damp conditions" (Eklektos et al., 2006: 498).

In a room in the National Museum of Natural History, where the Smithsonian stores its mummified remains, there is an individual who was unintentionally mummified in the 18th century in Philadelphia. The mummification occurred due to conditions within his casket. There have also been numerous reports of mummified brain tissue found in skulls. In some cases, "the preserved brain tissue persists even after the cranial bone has decomposed" (Eklektos et al., 2006: 499). Such cases of mummification have been documented in the deserts of Chile, in mass graves in Bulgaria, and in Denmark, among other places.

Both of the above-mentioned types of mummification, the incidental and the purposeful, are called *miira* in Japanese, a term adopted from the Portuguese language. However, individuals that have mummified themselves cannot be called *miira*. This type of mummification is unique. It is known as *sokushinbutsu:* becoming a Buddha in this very body.

Buddhism originated in the 6th century B.C.E. with a prince named Siddharta Gautama, also known as Sakyamuni (*Shaka Nyorai* in Japanese), which means Sage of the Sakya Tribe. His father was the ruler of a chiefdom in the Himalayan foothills in present-day Nepal. At the age of 29, he left his worldly belongings behind with the desire to attain Enlightenment. He became an ascetic, practicing self-torture and religious austerities for six years. Finally, he abandoned these practices, and in deep meditation, discovered the Middle Way, the Four Noble Truths, and the Noble Eight-fold Path to end suffering. He is known as the historical Buddha, Shaka Nyorai.

From India, "Buddhism was first brought to China at the behest of Emperor Ming (r. 58-75 C.E.) of the Han Dynasty, who had a dream of a radiant golden figure flying through the air. One of his advisors identified the image as the Buddha, a divine being from the western regions. Thereupon Emperor Ming dispatched an embassy to India that returned with a Buddhist scripture, two translators, and the famous Udayana image regarded by Buddhists as the first likeness ever made of Sakyamuni" (Sharf, 2001: 1).

Buddhism was introduced to Japan by the Koreans in the early half of the sixth century, and received official government support in 587 (Walthall, 2006: 18). Emperor Temmu (r. 672-686) and Empress Jito (r. 686-692) built temples in the capital[3] and in the provinces. They oversaw Buddhist ceremonies, sutra copying, and purification rituals. Emperor Shomu (r. 724-749) continued to promote Buddhist teachings throughout the country. "He ordered sutra readings at temples, austerities such as cold water baths at Shinto shrines, and the construction of religious structures. Following the Hayato Rebellion in 741, he ordered each province to build a seven-storied pagoda, a guardian temple, and a nunnery" (Walthall, 2006: 18).

By the eighth century, Buddhism had become commonplace, and it began to converge with the native religions of Japan. Numerous Buddhist sects were created, many worshipping different Buddhas (Jp. *Nyorai*) and Bodhisattvas (Jp. *Bosatsu*). Such sects included Tendai Buddhism, introduced by Saicho (766-822), and Shingon Buddhism, founded by Kukai (774-835), known posthumously as Kobo Daishi.

The tradition of self-mummification can be traced to Kukai, and the rationale for sokushin jobutsu, becoming a living Buddha, can be found in the teachings of Shingon.

Kobo Daishi and Shingon Buddhism

At nineteen years of age, near Daianji, one of the largest temples in Nara, the man who would become the monk Kukai (a.k.a. Kobo Daishi) asked a passing monk to explain the teachings of Buddhism. The monk taught him something, but it had nothing to do with Buddhist philosophy. It was a type of mnemonic device called "mantra-reciting for invoking Akasagarbha" or *gumonjiho* in Japanese. Akasagarbha (Jp. Kokuzo) is the name of a Bodhisattva who is the essence of all universal phenomena. The technique Kukai learned required chanting the mantra[4] one million times within one hundred consecutive days in a holy place. It also required complex ritual procedures including drawing an image of the Bodhisattva, construction of an altar, and memorization of complex *mudras* (hand-positions) for use in the meditation ritual. "While practicing this ascetic discipline again and again, a certain stratum dormant in human consciousness would awaken and begin to produce a mystical illumination by which one would be able to memorize whatever one reads in Buddhist scriptures" (Shiba, 2003: 43).

The monk was not so forthcoming regarding the location of the holy place. "That," he said, "you will have to find on your own."

Left: Statue of Kukai located outside of Taya Cave at Josen Temple (near Kamakura, Japan). Right: Statue of Vairocana at Todai Temple in Nara, Japan. Photographs courtesy of Ken Jeremiah.

Kukai wandered around searching for an area that he believed to be holy. He climbed mountains, visited temples, and explored caves. On the island of Shikoku, Kukai found a cave at the Cape of Muroto, where he felt a strong, spiritual presence. He meditated intently within the cave until he had an unusual experience. The morning star he had fixed his eyes upon suddenly rushed toward him, and he saw within a figure of Akasagarbha surrounded by a halo. It was most likely at this moment that Kukai became Buddhist, and he devoted himself entirely to understanding its subtlest teachings.

During the next several years, Kukai studied intently in temple libraries. He read ten thousand Buddhist scriptures (Shiba, 2003: 61) in all categories of the three vehicles, the five vehicles, and the three divisions of both Theravada and Mahayana scripture, but still he was not content. He knew that he was missing something, that the true nature of reality was not revealed in the exoteric texts that he had been studying.

At Todai Temple in Nara,[5] Kukai prayed in front of the giant statue of the Buddha Vairocana for assistance. Eventually, a figure approached him in a dream and said, "You are searching for the *Mahavairocana Sutra*."

Upon awakening, he immediately left his home and searched for the scroll in nearby temple libraries. Eventually, he found it in the basement of the east pagoda of Kumedera (a temple in Yamato

Province), located south of Nara near Kashiwara Palace. Kukai studied the sutra incessantly, but he could not understand it. He felt that the truth he sought was right in front of him, but he did not know how to extract it. For this knowledge, he traveled to China and studied esoteric Buddhism under the tutelage of a priest named Huiguo for several years. There he leaned Sanskrit mantras, mudras, and visualization of the sacred images of the yogic teachings of the *Mahavairocana Sutra*. His time spent in China removed all doubts and delusions, and when he returned to Japan, he began preaching a new type of Buddhism: Shingon, also known as *mikkyo* (secret teachings).

Before Kukai returned from China, all forms of Buddhism in Japan traced their beginnings to Sakyamuni, but Shingon's teachings claimed a direct descent from the cosmic Buddha Mahavairocana[6] (Dainichi Nyorai), the embodiment of the Universe itself.

"Kukai declared that his esoteric Buddhism was the direct manifestation of the teaching of the cosmic Buddha Mahavairocana and that the meditative practices prescribed in Esoteric Buddhist scriptures enabled one to attain enlightenment instantaneously" (Abe, 1999: 10). In Shingon faith, the attainment of complete Enlightenment, Buddhahood, is not a one-time historic event that occurred in the past. Rather, it is a science of spiritual discipline and ascetic practice that, when done correctly, can lead one to perfect awakening and absolute extinction of desires, becoming a Buddha in this lifetime.

Since Dainichi Nyorai is the embodiment of the Universe itself, all elements of nature are within him. Therefore, everything in nature, from stars and planets above to insects and pebbles below, possess Buddha nature. Man too has this Buddha nature. If he can eliminate desire and illusion, he will be able to perceive this Buddha nature in all things, and thereby understand the great function of the cosmic order. This is explained in the *Avatamsaka Sutra*: "The body of Buddha is inconceivable. In his body are all sorts of lands of sentient beings. Even in a single pore are countless vast oceans" (10: 32).

"Even in a single pore are inconceivable many lands, countless as particles of dust, inhabited by all sorts of living beings. In each of these numerous lands, there resides Vairocana Buddha, who expounds the excellent teaching amidst a great assembly of disciples. In every particle of dust in these lands, one also differentiates countless lands, some small, others large. In every particle of dust of these lands, too, one finds Vairocana Buddha" (10: 36).

Buddha nature is within man, so searching for Buddha is to search within oneself. This is the philosophy behind meditation and ascetic practices. Kukai once said, "If you realize what your mind truly is, then you understand the mind of Buddhas. If you realize the mind of the Buddhas, then you understand the mind of sentient beings. Those who realize the oneness of these three minds—the minds of practitioners, Buddhas, and sentient beings—are perfectly enlightened" (Abe, 1999: 128).

In Shingon belief, since all elements of nature are divine, manipulation of the elements in a prescribed manner can give a practitioner divine or supernatural powers. Any act, such as the use of secret hand positions, the intonation of mantras, language of the gods, drawing a sacred diagram of cosmic realms, or performing a divinely inspired ritual may result in mysterious powers if done correctly.

Throughout history, saints and sages have warned that the ultimate truth of existence, the nature of reality, and the nature of divine beings cannot be grasped by reading texts. Such things cannot be expressed in words. Shingon Buddhism teaches esoteric rites that will enable the practitioner (Jp. *ubasoku*) with true purpose to attain knowledge of the infinite. The practices enable people to attain Buddhahood in this very body, without having to die (Walthall, 2006: 33).

In order to attain this knowledge and gain divinely inspired powers, one had to conduct these rites in holy places and in a prescribed manner. Most often, aspirants would seclude themselves from society and perform austerities in caves or on sacred mountains. Famous martial artists throughout history have engaged in similar practices. Swordsman Bokuden Tsukahara confined himself in Kashima Shrine for 1,000 days of meditation and prayer before creating the Shinto Ryu, a sword art allegedly created with divine assistance (Sugawara, 1985: 25). Aikido founder Ueshiba Morihei, at age forty-two, disappeared into the mountains of Kumano for extended periods of time training in Kuki Shin Ryu, a martial art devised by mountain ascetics (Stevens, 1987: 70), and Miyamoto Musashi spent much of his later years meditating in a cave on Mount Iwato called Reigan (Wilson, 2004: 147).

Kukai spent a large portion of his life performing such austerities. "High in the mountains, on steep cliffs, in rocky gorges and on solitary shores, he lived by himself and, free of care, persevered in his strenuous training regime" (Abe, 1999: 76). The practices performed included starvation for periods of twenty-one days, meditation in deep caves in complete darkness, and meditation under waterfalls in the middle of winter. These practices are called *shugyo* in Japanese, and the practitioners that undertake them are known as *shugenja* or *yamabushi*. Such practices continue today.

Kukai carried such austerities into death. He was buried alive in a secluded cave on Mount Koya in 835. Before beginning his eternal meditation, he addressed his followers in the temple on Mount Koya. "At first I thought that I should live until a hundred years old and convert all the people, but now that you are all grown up there is no need for my life to be prolonged, and I shall leave for the Eternal Samadhi on the twenty-first day of next month, March of 835. But you need by no means grieve, for my spiritual force will still be alive here. Even after entering into the eternal meditation, I will save all sentient beings, accompanied by Maitreya[7] Bodhisattva in the Tusita Heaven. Surely, I will return here again with the Bodhisattva, 5.6 million years later [sic]. Until you cease your suffering on earth, I will carefully watch you and save you from such suffering" (Miyata, 2006: 31).

Statue of Maitreya, the Buddha of the future, that will save all sentient beings (Aomori, Japan). Photograph courtesy of Ken Jeremiah.

Many years after Kukai had entered into eternal samadhi, his disciples opened the cave to view his body. His hair had continued to grow after his death and was nearly three feet long. They shaved his head and changed his clothes, sealing the cave as they left, never to return again. Decades later, Kanken, one of his followers, returned to the cave. "When Kanken opened the cave, he was met by a thick cloud of dust. When the dust cleared, he saw that it had been from Kobo Daishi's robe, which had disintegrated and been swept up by the wind as he opened the cave. Kobo Daishi's hair was a foot long [apparently still growing since previously shaved]. Kanken, who had washed and put on a fresh robe beforehand,[8] shaved the saint's head once more with a new razor. The cord of the saint's crystal rosary had rotten away, and the beads lay scattered before him. Kanken gathered them up, strung them on a new cord, and put the rosary back in Kobo Daishi's hand. Finally, he dressed the saint in a new robe. As he left the cave he wept, overcome by a feeling of deep personal loss" (Tyler, 1987: 36).

Shugenja and Dewa Sanzan

Shugendo is a religious tradition found within sects of esoteric Buddhism. Its followers, known as *shugenja* or *yamabushi*, gain supernatural powers through ascetic practices on mountains or in caves. According to the doctrine of Shugendo, the goal of such austerities is to become a Buddha in one's human body. "In other words, the purpose of mountain austerities is to transform a profane man into a sacred man by mystic training at a sacred mountain" (Miyake, 2001: 78).

Mountains have always been regarded as spiritual places in Japan. They are the dwelling place of deities and ancestral spirits. In ancient Japan, tombs were built on mountains, and in the modern Japanese language, a burial procession is called *yamayuki*, which literally translates as "going to the mountain." Mountains are a transitory space between the secular world and the heavenly realms. "The mountain is an avenue to heaven; a mountain cave is an entrance to the otherworld. Therefore, the living beings on a mountain also have a liminal character. To be more exact, they have both a sacred and a profane character. A long-nose genie (*tengu*),[9] a demon (*oni*), and also a yamabushi—all of which reside on the mountain—share this liminal character" (Miyake, 2001: 79). Yamabushi, by engaging in the practice of austerities, change their state of existence. They become heavenly beings in between humans and gods. In Christian tradition, this is the same as a profane man becoming a saint within his lifetime

Dainichi Nyorai is the embodiment of the Universe and the principal deity of Shugendo. All parts of his body, therefore, are divine principles of nature that appear in all things, from Buddhas and Bodhisattvas, to humans and animals. So, humans have the same nature as Dainichi Nyorai, the cosmos itself, and all other Buddhist deities. When a yamabushi enters the sacred realm of the mountain and becomes aware of his Buddha nature, through asceticism, he can attain Buddhahood.

The performance of austerities is not easy. During winter, they meditate under cold waterfalls and fast for many days. They confine themselves in caves and meditate in complete darkness, sometimes seeing visions of gods or supernatural beings within. An example of such austere training is found in the *Heike Monogatari* ("The Tale of the Heike"), written in the 13th century. A man named Mongaku, the son of Watanabe Mochito, became a Buddhist. He shaved his head and began practicing austerities.

In Nachi (Kumano) there is a famous waterfall.[10] Mongaku decided to stand under it and repeat the invocation to Fudo Myo-o three hundred thousand times as a religious exercise.[11] He arrived at the waterfall in December. The river was frozen solid, and the waterfall was a mass of large icicles. Mongaku, invoking the power of Fudo Myo-o, immersed himself up to the neck and began chanting. However, after five days, he lost consciousness and his body drifted downstream, washing up onto the ice that encased the river. A boy found his body and dragged him away from the water. Others who were in the area started a fire to warm him, and Mongaku eventually regained consciousness. When he had recovered, he returned to the waterfall where he began his training again.

He again meditated under the freezing waters of Nachi Falls. On the third day, he lost consciousness again, and died. Two heavenly youths descended from above and awakened him. "We are Kongara and Seitaka, the messengers of Fudo Myo-o," the two youths said, "and we have come in obedience to the command of the Myo-o: 'Mongaku has made a sublime vow and is now undergoing unparalleled austerities; save him.'"

Then Mongaku asked, "Where is the abode of the Myo-o?"

"His abode is in the Tosotten, the fourth Heaven of Desire," they replied as they disappeared into the clouds. Mongaku exclaimed, "Now I am full of hope. Fudo Myo-o himself knows of my austerities." Again, he stood beneath the waterfall. This time he received the assistance of the Guardian King, and he was able to endure his austere training for three full weeks, feeling neither cold nor strain. After, it was said that he was strong and wise enough to pray a bird out of the sky (Sadler, 1972: 77-82).

Shugenja often worship Fudo Myo-o during their austere training. Fudo Myo-o is neither a Buddha nor a Bodhisattva. Rather, he is one of the five guardian kings of Buddhism, and a messenger of the cosmic Buddha Dainichi Nyorai. The fact that he is not a god makes him more accessible to men. Just as some Christians worship Jesus (the son), rather than God (the father), through austerities, practitioners can commune with Fudo Myo-o more easily than they can call upon Dainichi Nyorai. Then, with the assistance of Fudo Myo-o, they can commune with Dainichi Nyorai himself.

Left: Statue of Fudo Myo-o (Aomori, Japan).
Right: Entrance to Taya Cave, hand-carved from hard clay
(Josen Temple Complex, Japan). Photograph courtesy of Ken Jeremiah.

Calling upon Fudo Myo-o, yamabushi often confined themselves to dark caves, some that they carved themselves. The largest handmade cave is called Taya, located just outside of Kamakura, Japan. It is nearly 5,000 feet in length, and it has seventeen exercise halls with high, dome-shaped ceilings decorated with Sanskrit letters and numerous statues (Jeremiah, 2006: 35). Other famous man-made caves include those at Yamadera Temple, founded in 860 by the priest Ennin. From the front gate to the main temple complex on top of the mountain are 1,110 steps, and the caves carved into the mountainside are still used by shugenja today.

Near Yamadera Temple, in Yamagata, are three of the most holy mountains in Shugendo, collectively called Dewa Sanzan. These are Hagurosan, Gassan, and Yudonosan. Daijuku Bosatsu Shinnyokai Shonin, the monk who buried himself alive and successfully mummified himself, performed austerities daily on Yudono Mountain, one of the three most sacred places in all of Japan.[12] In ancient times, Yudonosan was called the unspeakable mountain, because no one was supposed to mention the name of the mountain or the name of the great spirit that resides there: Yudonosan Daigongen. On the mountain is a temple called Dainichibo,[13] where the body of Shinnyokai rests. It was founded in 807, by Kukai, and its chief priesthood covers 95 generations. The temple was used for worship by the Tokugawa Shogunate, and it is known as one of the holiest temples in northern Japan (Tohoku).

Shinnyokai used this temple as a base as he strove for enlightenment. Born in Asahi Village, in Etchuyama, he turned to Buddhist teachings at a young age, and only became more devoted as he grew older. In his twenties, he decided to become a living Buddha, and he began training in austerities. He continued his difficult training regimen for over seventy years. At age 96, he was buried alive, aspiring to become an attendant of Maitreya in the Tusita Heaven.

Other Self-Mummified Monks

Near Dainichibo and the mummified remains of Shinnyokai is a temple called Churenji which houses another self-made mummy, named Tetsumonkai Shonin. Tetsumonkai also spent years engaged in ascetic practices in the mountains, and he too successfully mummified himself by means of spiritual discipline and a special diet. Before burying himself alive, he cut out his own left eye and threw it in the Sumida River, praying for a cure for the eye-illnesses that were causing blindness in Edo at the time. In 1892, he entered Churen Temple to become a living Buddha. Other mummies in Japan include Tenko Myokai Shonin, who resides in Zokoin Temple, and Shungi Shonin, in Myoho Temple, who immortalized himself in 1686. Arisada Honin, a follower of the Buddha Yakushi Nyorai, sealed himself in his stone coffin in 1683, and he now holds a seat of honor at Kanshu Temple. There are approximately twenty self-mummified individuals in Japan, most of which are located around the holy trio of mountains: Dewa Sanzan, in Yamagata Prefecture.

Similar mummies exist outside of Japan as well. In the mountains of Tibet, 12,000 feet above sea level, there is an individual who mummified himself in 1475, and his remains still show no signs of decay. Locals worship him as a god. "There are numerous records of eminent Chinese monks whose bodies miraculously showed no trace of decay after death. For months and years following their decease their unembalmed bodies continued to bear a healthy and lifelike countenance and give off sweet perfume" (Sharf, 1992: 7).

In China, the successful mummification of a Chan (Jp. Zen) priest is considered proof of his spiritual attainment. The Buddhist priest Shan Wuwei died in 735, but he was not buried until 740. His body showed no sign of decay in the five-year interval between his death and his burial at Kuang Hua Monastery. "Eighteen years later, his tomb was opened by his disciples and his body recovered. Although the body had darkened in color and diminished in size, it remained well preserved and became the focus of a local cult, attracting the support of the Emperor himself" (Sharf, 1992: 8). Hundreds of similar cases are found throughout Asia, and there are many cases in China of crypt doors opening on their own only to reveal the unblemished, preserved remains of a Buddhist priest who had died years before. One famous case is the body of the fourth Chan patriarch, Daoxin, whose stupa doors opened by themselves, revealing his completely preserved body (Faure, 1998: 786).

When the priest Hui Shih was nearing death, he purified himself and did not eat. He sat in upright posture and died surrounded by his followers. The body was left there for ten days, as was the custom, and it remained seated in formal posture without change. His skin did not get pale, and he looked as though still alive. Ten years after his burial, the government declared that no bodies should be buried within the city walls, and several men decided to move his body to a grave south of the city. When they opened the tomb, he was still seated upright, as though in meditation, and his body had yet to decompose (Sharf, 1992: 20-21).

Sealing the Tomb

When the tomb was sealed, and the practitioner of Shugendo awaited his death, he awaited his rebirth as a Buddha. Herein lies a great paradox behind the practice of self-mummification. In order to attain Buddhahood, all desires must be extinguished, including the desire for Buddhahood itself. When there is nothing left, the truth will be revealed, but any desire or attachment, including the desire to become a sokushinbutsu, is a deterrent, and therefore abhorred.

It was important for the ascetic to eliminate desire, including the desire to self-mummify. This was difficult, since they prepared for their deaths for at least ten years and they engaged in practices that would help them to successfully mummify. However, mummification itself was not the goal. The true goal was to help all living creatures by serving Maitreya, the Buddha of the future. Their goal is a selfless one. Mummification, simply a means to this end, must also be a selfless act. The ascetic must eliminate selfhood and engage in such practices only to serve others.

The historical Buddha attained *nirvana*, often translated as a blissful and heavenly place. However, the term means "annihilation," and it refers to annihilation of the self. Buddhist ideas came from Indian religious beliefs, and in Hinduism, as in Buddhism, rebirth is a fact of nature. The only means of escaping the cycle of rebirth is the absolute disintegration of the self. Annihilation of Buddha makes his eternal presence in this world possible, for without self, no one can be reborn.

A *Bodhisattva* is another sort of Buddhist divinity who, rather than completely give up his body and life in exchange for Buddhahood, chooses to remain behind to assist others, but he still has to escape the cyclical rebirth of mortals. In Shugendo, the spirit is important. The physical body is not. However, the body has to be preserved, since successful preservation after death demonstrates the spiritual attainment of the being within.

The way a person dies is often indicative of the way in which he lived. In Japan, great strides were made in perfecting the art of death. Samurai had complex rituals for disemboweling themselves, composing a death poem just moments before. Witnesses would judge the man, based on his calmness, the steadiness of his hand as he wrote his last words, and the courage displayed as he dragged a knife through his abdomen (Turnbull 1977: 48, Shimabukuro and Pellman 1995: 124). Zen priests, too, had a prescribed way of dying. They called their disciples together and announced the time and place of their own natural passing. Like the samurai, they also wrote death poems, and on many occasions, they died sitting upright.

However, once a person is dead, the method of death will be forgotten in time. All creatures, whether enlightened sages or ignorant fools, will leave behind a corpse. Few may be mummified, the others will decay and disappear. Perhaps the mummified remains on display in temples in Japan only serve to remind visitors of the transitory nature of life, and of the inevitability of death. One cannot truly live, until one has faced the certainty of death.

Conclusion

After a decade of preparing for death, sustained by twigs and berries alone, engaged in constant ascetic practices, the sokushinbutsu looked as though already dead. He was in a transient state between life and death, following an extraordinary path. Rather than change his mind during ten grueling years of starvation and tortuous practices, he only became more devoted to his goal, and more fanatical in his beliefs.

This is not unlike the mind of a warrior. A samurai named Nabeshima Aki no kami Shigetake said that martial valor is found within fanaticism (Yamamoto, 1979: 84). Whole-hearted devotion to the Way leads to martial proficiency and eliminates discrimination between gain and loss, and life and death: the source of fear.

The warrior must embrace death. "There is a saying of the elders' that goes, 'Step from under the eaves and you are a dead man. Leave the gate and the enemy is waiting.' This is not a matter of being careful, it is to consider oneself as dead beforehand" (Yamamoto, 1979: 164).

Becoming a Living Buddha by means of self-mummification is illegal and no longer occurs in Japan. It is a thing of the past. However, like the mummified bodies that do not decay and will not disappear, the lessons of such individuals have been passed down to the present day. Single-minded determination, the complete absence of fear, and the nonexistence of self are demonstrated in the actions of these individuals, and they are the same qualities that are found in any master of the martial arts.

> "After I am no more,
> My home is still on Mount Koya.
> While my mind will be eased
> in the Tusita Heaven,
> I will check your devotional faith.
> Without ceasing my appearance on this earth,
> Especially at the Sacred Places:
> Where I was born…
> took esoteric discipline…
> Attained enlightenment…
> and where I entered into the Samadhi…"
> – Kobo Daishi

NOTES

1. The religious teachings found within Aikido are derived from Omoto Kyo, a Shinto-based faith founded by Nao Deguchi in 1892.
2. The Sengoku Jidai began around 1467 (with the onset of the Onin War, in Kyoto) and ended around 1590 when Toyotomi Hideyoshi re-unified the country.
3. The capital of Japan was Fujiwara at this time. In 710, the capital was moved to Nara, where it remained until 794. Then it was relocated to Heian-kyo, modern day Kyoto, where it remained until 1868. Finally, the capital was moved to modern day Tokyo.
4. The mantra of Akasagarbha is *Namu akasa garbhaya om arika mari muri svaha* ("So this is the means in which nature expresses its essence").
5. Completed in 752, Todai Temple is the largest wooden building in the world, and it houses the largest statue of Buddha in Japan (53 ft. high, weighing 452 tons).
6. Identified as the Dharmakaya itself, the Truth-Body of the Buddha.
7. According to scripture, 5,670,000 years after the death of Shaka Nyorai, after six cycles of existence, Maitreya (Jp. Miroku) will be born on this earth to save 9,600,000 people, then 9,400,000 people, and finally 9,200,000 people.
8. Japanese Buddhism, influenced by the native Shinto religion, requires practitioners to be clean, physically and spiritually, before completing any religious act. They must be free from all defilements.
9. Tengu are mythical half-man, half-bird creatures that live among pines and cryptomeria trees near mountain temples. The most recent report of a tengu spotting was by British anthropologist Carmen Blacker, in 1963, on Mount Kurama, Japan (Wilson, 2006: 20).
10. The water falls from a height of 133 meters (436 feet).
11. The invocation to Fudo Myo-o is *naama kusaa mandaaba saranankan* in Japanese.
12. The other two are Ise and Kumano.
13. The proper name for Dainichibo Temple is Yudonosan Ryusuiji Kongoin.

BIBLIOGRAPHY

ABE, R. (1999). *The weaving of mantra: Kukai and the construction of esoteric Buddhist discourse*. New York: Columbia University Press.

ANESAKI, M. (1999). *History of Japanese religion*. Tokyo: Charles E. Tuttle.

BAHN, P. AND RENFREW, C. (1996). *Archaeology: Theories, methods and practice*. New York: Thames and Hudson.

BARBOZA, D. (2006). China turns out mummified bodies for display. *New York Times* (8 August).

BINGENHEIMER, M. (2005). Roushen pusa and corpus integrum – Whole body relics in Buddhism and Christianity. Proceedings of The Contribution of Buddhism to World Culture. Mumbai: Somaiya Publications.

BLACKER, C. (1975). *The catalpa bow*. London: George Allen and Unwin.

BODIFORD, W. (1993). *Soto Zen in medieval Japan*. Honolulu: University of Hawaii Press.

BOISSELIER, J. (1994). *The wisdom of the Buddha*. New York: Harry N. Abrams.

BUNCE, W. (1955). *Religions in Japan*. Rutland, Vermont: Charles E. Tuttle.

CHOZANSHI, I. (2006). *The demon's sermon on the martial arts*. Tokyo: Kodansha.

CRAIG, A. (2003). *The heritage of Japanese civilization*. Upper Saddle River, New Jersey: Prentice Hall.

DAVID, R. AND ARCHBOLD, R. (2000). *Conversations with mummies*. New York: William Morrow.

DESHIMARU, T. (1985). *Questions to a Zen master*. New York: Penguin.

DINGM E-YOUNG, J. AND TAYLOR, E. (1998). Meditation as a voluntary hypometabolic state of biological estivation. *News in Physiological Sciences, 13*(3): 149-153.

EBREY, P. (1993). *Chinese civilization*. New York: Free Press.

EBREY, P. (1996). *China*. New York: Cambridge University Press.

EKLEKTOS, N., DAYAL, M. AND MANGER, P. (2006). A forensic case study of a naturally mummified brain from the Bushveld of South Africa. *Journal of Forensic Sciences,* (51): 498.

FAURE, B. (1998). The Buddhist icon and the modern gaze. *Critical Inquiry, 24*(46): 768-813.

FRIDAY, K. (1997). *Legacies of the sword*. Hawaii: University of Hawaii Press.

GOEPPER, R. (1993) *Aizen Myoo: The esoteric king of lust*. Zurich: Artibus Asiae, Museum Rietberg.

HAKEDA, Y. (Trans). (1972). *Kukai: Major works*. New York: Columbia University Press.

HITOSHI, M. (2001). *Shugendo: Essays on the structure of Japanese folk religion*. Michigan: Ann Arbor Center for Japanese Studies, The University of Michigan.

HOFFMAN, Y. (Ed). (1986). *Japanese death poems*. Tokyo: Tuttle Publishing.

JEREMIAH, K. (2006). Taya cave. *Kansai Time Out,* (352): 35.

KATO, B., TAMURA, Y., AND MIYASAKA, K. (Trans). (2003). *The threefold lotus sutra*. Tokyo: IBC Publishing.

KIM, Y. (1973). *Oriental thought*. Maryland: Littlefield, Adams Quality Paperbacks.

KIYOTA, M. (1967). Presuppositions to the understanding of Japanese Buddhist thought. *Monumenta Nipponica, 22*(4): 251-259.

MIYATA, T. (2006). *A Henro pilgrimage guide to the 88 temples of Shikoku Island, Japan*. Los Angeles: Koyasan Buddhist Temple.

MORREL, R. (1987). *Early Kamakura Buddhism: A minority report*. Berkeley: Asian Humanities Press.

MURPHEY, R. (2004). *East Asia: A new history*. New York: Pearson Longman.

NEWMAN, C. (2005). The monk who embalmed himself. *National Geographic*, (207): 5.

RAVINA, M. (2004). *The last samurai: The life and battles of Saigo Takamori*. New Jersey: John Wiley and Sons.

SADLER, A. (Trans). (1972). *The ten foot square hut and Tales of the Heike*. Tokyo: Tuttle Publishing.

SANGHARAKSHITA (Trans). (2001). *Dhammapada*. New York: Barnes and Noble.

SHARF, R. (1992). The idolization of enlightenment: on the mummification of Ch'an masters in medieval China. *History of Religion, 32*(1): 1-31.

SHARF, R. AND SHARF, E. (Trans). (2001). *Living images: Japanese Buddhist icons in context*. Stanford: CA: Stanford University Press.

SHIMABUKURO, M. AND PELLMAN, L. (1995). *Flashing steel: Mastering Eishin-Ryu swordsmanship*. Berkley, CA: Frog, Ltd.

SMALL, L. (2004). Fascinating relics. *Smithsonian, 34*(10): 10.

SOCIETY FOR THE PROMOTION OF BUDDHISM. (1998). *The teaching of Buddha*. Tokyo: Bukkyo Dendo Kyokai.

STEVENS, J. (1989). *Abundant peace*. Boston: Shambala.

SUGAWARA, M. (1985). *Lives of master swordsmen*. Tokyo: East Publications.

SUNADOMARI, K. (2004). *Enlightenment through aikido*. Berkeley, CA: North Atlantic Books.

TAKAMURA, Y. (1999). An interview with Takamura Yukiyoshi. *Aikido Journal, 26*(2): 22-33.

THURMAN, R. (Trans). (1994). *Tibetan book of the dead*. New York: Bantam.

TURNBULL, S. (2005). *Warriors of medieval Japan*. New York: Osprey Publishing.

TURNBULL, S. (1977). *The samurai: A military history.* New York: MacMillen Publishing.
TYLER, R. (Trans). (1987). *Japanese tales.* New York: Pantheon Books.
UESHIBA, M. (1991). *Budo.* Tokyo: Kodansha.
VISSER, M. (1935). *Ancient Buddhism in Japan.* Leiden: E.J. Brill.
WALTHALL, A. (2006). *Japan: A cultural, social, and political history.* New York: Houghton Mifflin.
WILSON, W. (2004). *The lone samurai.* Tokyo: Kodansha.
YAGYU, M. (2003). *The life giving sword.* Tokyo: Kodansha.
YAMAMOTO, T. (1979). *Hagakure.* Tokyo: Kodansha.

JAPANESE KANJI GLOSSARY

Churenji	注連寺
Daijuku Bosatsu Shinnyokai Shonin	代受苦菩薩真如海上人
Dainichi Nyorai	大日如来
Dainichibo	大日坊
Fudo Myo-o	不動明王
Fujiwara	藤原
Gumonjiho	求聞持法
Kobo Daishi	弘法大師
Kukai	空海
Miira	ミイラ
Mikkyo	密教
Miroku	彌勒
Nyorai	如来
Oni	鬼
Shingon	真言
Shugyo	修行
Shugenja	修験者
Sokushinjobutsu	即身成仏
Sokushinbutsu	即身仏
Tengu	天狗
Tetsumonkai Shonin	鉄門海上人
Yamabushi	山伏
Yamayuki	山行き
Zen	禅

chapter 8

Psychology, Physical Disability, and the Application of Buddhist Mindfulness to Martial Arts Programs

by Mark D. Kelland, Ph.D.

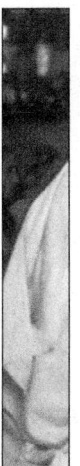

Introduction

People with physical disabilities face unique challenges in life. Indeed, those challenges are likely to be unique for each person with a disability. One of the most serious concerns is social isolation, which is a common sign of psychological disorder. For people with disabilities, social isolation often arises externally, due to the stigma associated with disability. Especially for children, the opportunity to play with other children is an important part of growing up, and this may be doubly difficult if the child is physically disabled and stigmatized. Buddha's teachings emphasize accepting ourselves as we are, both body and mind, and letting go of our attachment to desires and expectations.

Thus, so-called "traditional" martial arts programs, those with an emphasis on values, integrity, and historical traditions, provide an ideal opportunity for people with disabilities. Not only are the martial arts a physical activity typically done in a group setting, they also routinely incorporate Buddhist philosophy. So a well designed martial arts program for people with disabilities can help them stay physically fit, meet new friends, and learn to accept themselves as they are, even as they strive to improve themselves.

Psychology and Physical Disability

Early psychological studies on people with disabilities emphasized a sociocultural approach, suggesting that personality exists within the context of an individual's relationships, and that expectations of body-image within that context are important (Barker et al., 1946; Pintner et al., 1941). Although these early studies found no predictable or inevitable psychological consequences of being disabled, certain types of problems were the most likely to occur. Children with disabilities fall into the roles expected of them due to cultural adaptations. For example, if the family of a child who is blind brings everything to them, the child becomes very egocentric, always expecting to be the center of attention, and focusing inward on themselves. Severe physical handicaps can be even more isolating, leading to withdrawal and a significant degree of social handicap. They might then lack initiative in school, leading to poor education despite their intellectual ability to perform well.

The factor that seemed to matter most in these studies was whether the family situation was conducive to healthy development. Whereas most children with disabilities were generally well adjusted, those with severe disabilities who were also overprotected and indulged by their family were the least likely to be well adjusted. Much worse, of course, are situations in which a disabled child is rejected or abused by their parent(s). Barker et al. (1946) share a poignant story in which a young girl was in the hospital for two months at the age of two. Her mother never visited her, and then her father blamed her for her brother's death, and he never paid attention to her again! This girl grew up with many psychological problems, but they could hardly be attributed solely to her physical disability.

Two early personality theorists who addressed these issues were Alfred Adler and Heinrich Meng (see Barker et al., 1946). Adler believed we are all born with feelings of inferiority, since babies are indeed helpless. We then strive for superiority, which is best accomplished through social interaction. Children born with a disability may find it more difficult to overcome their feelings of inferiority. Someone who becomes disabled may re-experience their infantile feelings of inferiority, and once again need to strive for superiority. This need for superiority can provide the energy to work hard in rehabilitation, but if feelings of inferiority overwhelm the individual, then an inferiority complex can arise.

Meng believed that the environment can be either a hazard or an advantage. If a child feels unloved, or if love has been withdrawn, the psychological consequences can be devastating. But the most serious problems arise if the child cannot play. This interferes with natural psychological development. This is one situation in which a martial arts program can be a wonderful opportunity. It is a structured environment which can provide appropriate physical activities and can be a lot of fun.

Broken & cold!
A photo by the author of a tree limb shattered by an ice storm.

Later, Beatrice Wright still found that "no matter how the studies are grouped, the data cannot be ordered so that scores of inferiority are in any systematic way related to disability or to such aspects of disability as type, duration, or degree" (1960: 52). She felt that the connection between feelings of inferiority and physical disability had been oversimplified. For example, a child with a mild disability might be expected to have an easier time adjusting. However, that child is almost normal, so they may try to hide their disability, thus avoiding the process of adjustment altogether. In contrast, a child with a severe disability must deal with it, and if they receive proper social support, they may adjust well.

In the 1970s, further studies found that people with physical disabilities were generally well adjusted psychologically, even during adolescence. Body-image can be critical to the psychological development of adolescents. McDaniel (1976) reported that disability or severe illness could interfere with the normal progress of adolescent development, but it did not affect personality per se. Disabled adolescents are also at greater risk for lower social status, lower self-esteem, and having an external locus of control, but these negative consequences can be ameliorated by the adolescent's intelligence, emotional maturity, and overall psychological adjustment.

When a person becomes disabled there is an initial sense of loss and grief. The ability to cope depends on the individual. Those who can embrace change, rather than resist it, score highest on measures of life satisfaction and self-esteem. The individual's values and goals are important as well (Vash, 1981). For example, an active, athletic individual is likely to be particularly intolerant of a sedentary lifestyle. For someone such as this, a martial arts program may be a good choice.

A question often asked following the occurrence of a disability is "Why me?" Spirituality offers answers beyond medical statistics or actuarial tables. One of the most important things that spirituality offers is hope. It can also infuse our lives with a larger, all-pervasive sense of meaning and purpose. In Western societies there is an emphasis on putting one's 'faith' in medicine. Vash (1981) suggests that an ideal situation would be one in which we combined Western medicine with Eastern spirituality.

Peterson and Seligman believe that spirituality "is the most human of the character strengths as well as the most sublime ... People with this strength have a theory about the ultimate meaning of life that shapes their conduct and provides comfort to them" (2004: 533). This quote fits well with the analysis of personality characteristics of martial artists conducted by Brandon Seig (2004). Seig found an association between 'traditional' martial arts training, with its emphasis on values and philosophy, and positive changes in personality development, particularly among delinquent youth.

Buddhist Mindfulness of Body

Mindfulness of the body is a first step toward letting go of one's attachments to all things, including our body and mind. But if we acknowledge pain and discomfort in our bodies, as is often the case for someone with a physical disability, it can be quite difficult to let go of it, even in order to be liberated from our suffering.

According to Andrew Olendzki (2008), the *Abhidhamma* describes mindfulness as more than just meditation. Meditation helps us get in touch with the initial point of each experience. Focusing intently and without interruption on the breath, for example, can lead to a deep state of meditation. But mindfulness is still something more; it is a wholesome state during which unwholesome states cannot arise. Included in the wholesome mental states are self-respect, respect for others, and faith. Mindfulness keeps the mind focused, and is caused by strong perception of the four foundations of mindfulness (mindfulness of body, feelings, consciousness, and mental objects):

> When true mindfulness arises, one feels as if one is stepping back and observing what is happening in experience, rather than being embedded in it. This does not mean separation or detachment, but is rather a sense of not being hooked by a desirable object or not pushing away a repugnant object.   – Olendzki, 2008: 55-56

It may seem that mindfulness is a difficult state to achieve, but the key is to continually cultivate and develop mindfulness. We can create favorable conditions when meditating mindfully, such as relaxing the body and focusing the attention softly. Being aware of one's body, accepting it as it is, and separating one's identity from the body can be very helpful. Observing your body during training, without being hindered by its limitations, can open your eyes to a whole new way of enjoying physical activity.

According to Jon Kabat-Zinn (1990), there is wisdom within the body, for those who are willing to experience their body, rather than just taking it for granted. As he points out, making a personal commitment to working with the very stress and pain that is causing suffering may be even more important for people with chronic illness or disability. It may be one way of regaining some control over the condition of your life. According to the Buddha:

> As he sat there, the housefather Nakulapitar addressed the Exalted One, saying: "Master, I am a broken-down old man, aged. . . I am sick and always ailing. . ."
> "True it is, true it is, housefather, that your body is weak and cumbered. Where, housefather, thus you should train yourself: "Though my body is sick, my mind shall not be sick."
>   – Kindred Sayings; Woodward, 1975: 1-2

Gautama Buddha went on to emphasize that everyone faces

challenges arising from their own bodies. He likened the senses to six animals: snake, crocodile, bird, dog, jackal, and monkey, each pulling in a different direction. In the *Connected Discourses on the Six Sense* Bases (*Salayatanasamyutta*), we learn to accept this reality, and train to work with it:

> "A strong post or pillar": this, *bhikkhus*, is a designation for mindfulness directed to the body. Therefore, bhikkhus, you should train yourselves thus: "We will develop and cultivate mindfulness directed to the body, make it our vehicle, make it our basis, stabilize it, exercise ourselves in it, and fully perfect it." Thus should you train yourselves (Bodhi, 2000: 1256-1257).

Mindfulness is important in every aspect of life, and every activity should be performed mindfully. One can be mindful of the entire body while just walking or while performing any of our daily tasks. It is not the activity that determines whether or not it should be done mindfully, we should live mindfully. Training body and mind together is essential for a person's full development:

> "If the body is unmastered, the mind will be unmastered; if the body is mastered, the mind is mastered."
> – the Buddha, cited in Nyanaponika, 1965: 105

Buddhism and the Martial Arts

Buddhism teaches non-violence. The Five Precepts begin with a command to abstain from killing. The Tiep Hien Order, founded by Thich Nhat Hanh (1987) and his colleagues during the Vietnam War, calls for both not killing and not allowing others to kill. How do we not allow others to kill? How do we protect other people who can not protect themselves? This is where martial arts training and Buddhism come together. According to legend, the Zen Buddhist monk Bodhidharma found the monks at Shaolin monastery in such poor physical condition that it interfered with their ability to meditate. So he developed a series of exercises that would both strengthen and steady their bodies for meditation and invigorate them afterward. In addition, they would be able to defend themselves and the temple (Ch'en, 1964, Fauliot, 2000). Although martial arts existed well before Bodhidharma's time, the value of this legend is its connection of the martial arts to a spiritual life and an emphasis on self-defense and non-violence.

It is in Bodhidharma's lesson *Hsieh Mai Lun,* or *Treatises on the Blood Lineage of True Dharma* (contained in Dukes, 1994), that we find a section entitled *Movement is the Source of No Mindedness.* The mind, he says, cannot be separated from the four elements of the physical body. When a person has trained their mind to recognize the true nature of Self (which is the Buddha mind), there is movement which immediately fulfills the intentions of the mind. This level of mind/body training would, indeed, create a formidable martial artist.

At the beginning of the 1900s, many martial arts masters were concerned about modernization and Westernization diluting the content of martial arts as mind/body training within a Buddhist tradition (Fauliot, 2000). The common term for Japanese martial arts had been *bujutsu,* but many masters wanted to emphasize the spiritual aspects of training by using the term *do,* or 'way.' Subsequently, jujutsu became judo, aikijutsu became Aikido, kenjutsu became kendo, etc. Judo and Aikido (along with taijiquan, Hapkido, and others) are often called 'soft' martial arts, yet they offer an excellent means of self-defense. The soft style of defending oneself is advocated in the *Daodejing* (Lao Tsu, 1989), and may be the ideal approach for people with disabilities.

Although Buddhism teaches non-violence, we live in a world that is all too often violent. How do we maintain our composure, even when faced with a potential threat? The answer is to cultivate mindfulness. Upasika Kee Nanayon (1995) describes the cultivation of mindfulness as a "battle within." To defeat one's enemies, the cravings and defilements in your own heart, you can not be weak or lax. But at the same time, you must gauge your strength, and find skillful ways of accomplishing this task. The mind must be centered and neutral, and we must fully and constantly train our mindfulness, so we do not lose control of our emotions. If we effectively use mindfulness to guard the actions of the mind at every moment, we will be able to probe and investigate each situation for insight before we act impulsively.

Martial Arts Programs for People with Physical Disabilities

Many martial arts schools accommodate individuals with physical disabilities. I will mention just a few formal programs I am familiar with. Two of them maintain websites and their programs are available on DVD. The others are only available to those who live near them, but the directors have been very gracious in sharing their experiences and expertise.

In 1996, Jurgen Schmidt established the International Disabled Self-Defense Association, following an alarming rise in crimes against people with disabilities. Schmidt has used a wheelchair since an armed assailant shot him in the back. Nonetheless, he continued his training, and earned a black belt in Hapkido. Based on the Combat Hapkido style, he developed DefenseAbility as an entirely self-defense based program for people in wheelchairs.

The DefenseAbility program is available on DVD, and the material is presented in an organized and thorough manner. Due to popular demand, there is now a system in place for awarding student ranks, and they have a certification program for instructors who are interested in learning and teaching DefenseAbility.

The Cane Masters International Association (CMIA) was founded by Mark Shuey, Sr. in the year 2000. CMIA provides high-quality canes (with self-defense features) and has a self-defense system for training with the cane and earning rank. The advantage of the cane is that it can be carried anywhere. Once again, the CMIA system is available on DVD, and the presentation is very clear. Although the lower rank tests can be videotaped, the rank of Canemaster must be earned in person.

The CMIA system isn't just for people with disabilities. Many people with injuries could use a cane rather than crutches, and many people use canes as they get older. Thus, the cane is an ideal self-defense weapon for anyone to learn.

In February, 2009, I had the pleasure of visiting Natural Motion Martial Arts in Scarborough, Maine, which specializes in providing martial arts training for people with physical disabilities. Shawn Withers is a stroke survivor, with significant left-side weakness, who began studying Shaolin Kenpo twelve years after his stroke. He now holds a 2nd degree Black Belt in that style, and the rank of Canemaster from the CMIA.

Although his Kenpo instructors were able to help Withers make adjustments to accommodate his weaker left side, the adjustments often either did not work well or were just too simplistic. Along with his wife,

Andrea Withers, they began their own dojo and developed a unique style, called Broken Wing Kenpo (Withers and Sims, 2007). Broken Wing Kenpo blends a variety of styles, and is adaptable to the abilities of each student. Andrea Withers has also developed a program for training martial arts instructors who work with people who have physical challenges (the term they prefer), based on what she calls the CRITICAL Approach™. I found this to be an impressively comprehensive program, including guidelines for initially meeting with prospective students, developing a plan for their training, assessing, re-evaluating, and correcting that plan, always remembering to have some fun and laugh.

Left: Shawn Withers demonstrating a cane self-defense technique against his assistant instructor John. Right: The author taking the C.R.I.T.I.C.A.L. Approach™ program developed and taught by Andrea Withers.
Photographs courtesy of M. Kelland.

Another program dedicated to working with people who are disabled is a joint venture between Thousand Waves Foundation and The Rehabilitation Institute of Chicago. Senpai Rebecca Angevine and Dr. Max Kuroda teach Adapted Seido Karate to students ranging in age from 5-19 years old. The range of motor skills varies from mild to severe, and some of the children have cognitive challenges as well. When I attended one of their classes it was amazing to see the commitment of the instructors and the enthusiasm of the students. Although very different types and levels of physical assistance were necessary for working with many of the students, overall, there was no difference between the class I attended and any other enthusiastic martial arts class.

I would be remiss if I failed to mention a program that has already appeared in the *Journal of Asian Martial Arts*. Dr. Anne Barnfield, a 4th degree Black Belt in Shorin Ryu Karate, runs an after-school Karate Club at the Robarts School for the Deaf in London, Ontario, Canada. I refer you to her article for an excellent description of the establishment and development of a karate club for Deaf children, with a traditional emphasis on body, mind, and spirit (Barnfield, 2004).

The stupa at Barre Center for Buddhist Studies (Massachusetts), which contains a relic of Sariputta, the first scholar of the Buddha's teachings. Photograph courtesy of M. Kelland.

Conclusions

Despite 60 years of research, psychologists have found no evidence for a 'psychology of disability,' whether a person is born disabled or acquires a disability later in life. What appears to be most important is the social support that the person with the disability receives. When problems do arise, social isolation is the most likely, particularly given the stigmatization of the disabled that continues in our society. For young children, the potential lack of opportunities to play may interfere with the normal process of growing up. These concerns can become quite serious if they converge on the challenging years of adolescence.

Traditional martial arts training offers numerous advantages for people with disabilities. It provides physical fitness training and it is typically done in a group setting. This provides opportunities to make new friends and meet a variety of people. If a program is designed carefully, a healthy dose of fun (i.e., play) can be included. Learning practical self-defense skills can help restore a sense of control within one's life. And the historical tradition of the martial arts, as well as the community of one's school, can offer a sense of identity which is especially important for adolescents.

As I met martial arts instructors working with students who are disabled, I was struck by how open, friendly, professional, and passionate they were about their work. Perhaps these are prerequisite personality traits for the kind of person who is willing and able to face this challenge. It is also likely that the experience of offering such a program to people with disabilities helps to nurture these traits in the instructors. Either way, there are some amazing people providing opportunities for those with disabilities to benefit from the physical, psychological, and spiritual aspects of traditional martial arts training.

> Practice and wisdom must exist side by side.
> For they are like the two wheels of a cart.
> Likewise, helping oneself and helping others
> Are like the two wings of a bird.
> – Wonhyo (617-686); cited in Do-young (2004)

BIBLIOGRAPHY

BARKER, R., WRIGHT, B., AND GONICK, M. (1946). *Adjustment to physical handicap and illness: A survey of the social psychology of physique and disability.* New York: Social Science Research Council.

BARNFIELD, A. (2004). Traditional martial arts with a non-traditional population: Teaching the Deaf. *Journal of Asian Martial Arts, 13*(4), 16-27.

BODHI, BHIKKHU (2000). *The connected discourses of the Buddha: A translation of the Samyutta Nikaya.* Boston, MA: Wisdom Publications.

CH'EN, K. (1964). *Buddhism in China: A historical survey.* Princeton, NJ: Princeton University Press.

DO-YOUNG (Ed.). (2004). *What is Korean Buddhism?* Seoul, Korea: Jogye Order of Korean Buddhism.

DUKES, T. (1994). *The Bodhisattva warriors: The origin, inner philosophy, history and symbolism of the Buddhist martial art within India and China.* York Beach, ME: Samuel Weiser.

FAULIOT, P. (2000). *Martial arts teaching tales of power and paradox: Freeing the mind, focusing chi, and mastering the self.* Rochester, VT: Inner Traditions.

KABAT-ZINN, J. (1990). *Full catastrophe living: Using the wisdom of your body and mind to face stress, pain, and illness.* New York, NY: A Delta Book.

LAO TSU (1989). *Tao te ching.* (English, J. and Feng, G., Trans.) New York: Vintage Books.

McDaniel, J. (1976). *Physical disability and human behavior, 2nd Ed.* New York, NY: Pergamon Press.

Nyanaponika, T. (1965). *The heart of Buddhist meditation.* York Beach, ME: Samuel Weiser.

Olendzki, A. (2008). The real practice of mindfulness. *Buddhadharma: The Practitioner's Quarterly, 7,* 50-57.

Peterson, C. and Seligman, M. (2004). *Character strengths and virtues: A handbook and classification.* New York: Oxford University Press.

Pintner, R., Eisenson, J., and Stanton, M. (1941). *The psychology of the physically handicapped.* New York: F. S. Crofts and Co.

Seig, B. (2004). Gravitation versus change: Explaining the relationship between personality traits and martial arts training. *Journal of Asian Martial Arts, 13*(3), 8-23.

Thich, Nhat Hanh (1987). *Interbeing: Commentaries on the Tiep Hien Precepts.* Berkeley, CA: Parallax Press.

Upasika Kee Nanayon (1995). *An unentangled knowing: The teachings of a Thai Buddhist lay woman.* Malaysia: Khao Suan Luang Dhamma Community.

Vash, C. (1981). *The psychology of disability.* New York: Springer Publishing Company.

Withers, S. and Sims, S. (2007). *Broken wing: You can't quit. Not ever. A true story of courage and inspiration.* Belfast, ME: Mystic Wolf Press.

Woodward, F. (1975). *The book of the Kindred Sayings (Sanyutta-Nikaya) or grouped suttas, Part III.* London, England: The Pali Text Society.

Wright, B. (1960). *Physical disability – A psychological approach.* New York: Harper and Row Publishers.

INDEX

Aikido, 92, 99, 108 note 1, 119
aikijutsu, 119
amulet, 60
ascetic discipline (*shugyo*), 92, 99
baguachang, 14, 36, 84-85
Baopuzi, 30, 35
bioenergy (*qi, ki*), 13-14, 26-30, 32, 34, 38 note 12, 40 note 38, 79, 81-82, 85-86, 91
Bodhidharma, 1-22, 77, 119
Bokuden Tsukahara, 92, 99
breathing practice, 13-15, 19, 26, 29-30, 32, 55, 60, 62, 81 note 4, 84
Buddhism, 1-13, 16-21, 30-31, 33, 39 note 24, 42, 46, 48, 50, 53, 55, 66-67, 74-75, 77, 92, 95-99, 101-102, 104-106, 108 note 8, 113-114, 116, 118-119
Cheng Zongyou, 73-75
Churen Temple, 104
Combat Hapkido, 120
Daian Temple, 96
Dainichibo Temple, 94, 104, 108 note 13
Daodejing, 82-83, 86, 119,
Daoism, 8, 26, 79-89
daoyin, 28-29, 32, 36, 81
DefenseAbility, 120
Dewa Sanzan, 101, 103-104
disabilities, 113-115, 119-120, 122-123
Drunken Eight Immortals, 73
eight trigrams (*bagua*), 84
Eighteen Luohan Hands, 14, 18-19, 21
Elucidation of Shaolin Staff Methods, 74-74
Enryaku Temple, 48-50
Epitaph to Wang Zhengnan, 72
external qigong, 14

fangshi, 31-33, 35, 39 note 26
Five Animal Games, 73, 81
five elements (*wuxing*), 26-27
Forest of Stupas, 71, 77
Fujiwara clan, 48-49
Guan Gong, 65-66
halberd, 65-67
Heaven and Earth Society, 73
Hinduism, 53-55, 57, 106
Hongquan, 73
horse-riding stance, 13, 21
Hua Tuo, 81
Huang Tuah, 60, 62 note 8
Hui Ke, 5, 8-12, 16, 18
Hui Neng, 17-18
immortals, 31-36, 40 note 38, 41 note 45, 73, 104
internal qigong, 14
International Disabled Self-Defense Association, 120
invulnerability, 60
Islam, 53, 55-57
jade, 28-29
Journey to the West, 66-67, 77
judo, 119
Kanshu Temple, 104
Kashima Shinto Ryu, 92
Kashima Shrine, 99
kebatinan, 53-62
kendo, 119
kenjutsu, 119
King Jinnaluo, 74-75
Kofuku Temple, 48-49
kris, 59-60, 62 note 8
Kuang Hua Monastery, 105
Kukai, 96-100, 104
Kumedera Temple, 97
kuntao, 57

Laixiangji, 32
Laozi, 31, 83
Liezi, 27
Mao Zedong, 80, 85, 88
Marrow Cleansing Classic (*Xisuijing*), 14-15, 18-19
Mojiaquan, 73
Miyamoto Musashi, 92, 99
Monkey Boxing, 71
Mount Wudang, 72
mudras, 96, 98
mummification, 93-96, 104-105, 107
Muscle Change Classic (*Yijinjing*), 14, 18-19
naginata, 46, 48, 51
Neo-Confucianism, 26, 35
Niten Ichi Ryu, 92
non-violence, 118-119
Omoto Kyo, 108
pendekar, 59-61, 62 note 7
pukulan, 57
Qi Jiguang, 73
qigong, 14, 26, 30, 32-33, 35-37, 38 note 13, 40 note 43, 43 note 63
samurai, 45-51, 77, 106-107
sanchin kata, 13
secret society, 73-74, 77
Shaolin staff, 73-75
Shaolin Temple, 1-2, 5, 7, 12, 16, 19-21, 85
Shen Guang, 8
Shindo Yoshin Ryu, 92
Shingon, 96, 98-99
Shinto, 96, 108 notes 1 and 8
Shinto Ryu, 99
Shorin Ryu Karate, 122
Shorinji Kempo, 15-16
Shugendo, 101, 103, 105-106
Siddharta Gautama, 95
silat, 53, 55, 57-61, 61 note 2, 62 note 4
Silat Seni Gayong, 61 note 2, 62 note 4

Six Harmonies Eight Methods (*liuhebafa*), 84-85
Song Mountain (*Songshan*), 7
Sword Hunt Edict, 51
taijiquan, 14, 36, 65, 79, 81, 83-85, 119
Taipingjing, 26-27, 31, 335
Taira clan, 50
The Tale of the Heike (*Heike Monogatari*), 102
Taoist Restoration Society, 81
tea, 7, 93
Tiep Hien Order, 118
Thich Nhat Hanh, 118
Todai Temple, 97, 108 note 5
Triads, 16-17, 73
Uechiryu, 13
Ueshiba Morihei, 92, 99
wall gazing (*biguan*), 3, 5-10, 13, 15, 19-20
White Lotus, 35, 42 notes 62 and 63, 75
wuwei, 83
xingyiquan, 65, 81, 84-85
Yagyu Shinkage Ryu, 92
Yamabushi, 92-93, 100-101, 103
Yamadera Temple, 103
yin-yang, 83
Yue Fei, 84
Zhang Daoling, 31
Zhang Sanfeng, 72, 79
Zhu Xi, 26
Zhuangzi, 28-29, 72, 82-83

Printed in Great Britain
by Amazon